Human Resource MANAGEMENT

DANTES/DSST* Study Guide

© 2016 Breely Crush Publishing, LLC

*DSST is a registered trademark of The Thomson Corporation and its affiliated companies, and does not endorse this book.

971110915143

Published by Breely Crush Publishing, LLC
10808 River Front Parkway
South Jordan, UT 84095
www.breelycrushpublishing.com

ISBN-10: 1-61433-163-4
ISBN-13: 978-1-61433-163-6

Printed and bound in the United States of America.

Table of Contents

Overview of Human Resources Field

What do human capital, intellectual assets, and key-person insurance all have in common? They show how important people are today in every aspect of running a business. Each person, whether they work on an assembly line in a factory, in a doctor's office or marketing department, has special knowledge that most likely, only they know. This gives them a value to business, which can sometimes seem cold-hearted. In business, the way to be successful is to have a competitive advantage. You gain a competitive advantage by having the best people. The best trained assistant can do twice as much work as a new person, five times more than a temp and ten times more than a high school graduate. Each person in your organization should contribute to and have their own bank of knowledge about how to do their job.

Each time you have to replace one of these people there are hidden costs. These costs are the productivity lost during the time the new person is trained until he or she is competent to the ability of the person being replaced. This shows you how valuable people are to a business or how detrimental the wrong person can be in time, money and mistakes.

That's where Human Resource Management comes in. They manage the company's most important resource or asset, the employees. Employees are only valuable if they are productive, efficient and perform their jobs well. These employees can perform tasks faster and better than anyone else around them. This is one way to recognize an asset. The term Human Resource Management can be cumbersome so we'll reduce it to HRM.

History of HR Management

HRM has been part of the business process since the first person sold anything for a profit. Think back to the time of the middle ages; masters of crafts such as blacksmithing, baking, painting, weaving, and so on, would take apprentices on for a fee. Over several years, these apprentices learned the craft while living with their master and working in return for education. Most of the time, the apprentices' families also paid the master for the privilege of the student learning from them. Apprentices experienced the same ups and downs due to the economy as their masters.

Once the industrial age began, this entire relationship changed. Factories sprung up, able to create items. These factories only required a low-skilled worker to do the same simple task over and over. Manual labor, not smarts and skill, was needed. Henry Ford is known for having wondered why workers brought their heads to work when all he needed was their hands and feet. These employees were interchangeable and the management knew they were easily replaceable. At the time, employers only worried about the speed with which the employees could create the products.

This all changed around the late 1800s. Employers were experiencing heavy turnover. The environment the employees were working in was unsafe; they worked too many hours; and for not enough pay. Disgruntled workers result in higher absenteeism and ultimately turnover. For the factory, this meant that productivity suffered. Workers began to form unions to negotiate for them. At what is believed to be the first company with a Human Resources Department, National Cash Register put together a group of people that would handle such issues as hiring, firing, problems with other employees or supervisors, etc. They also handled safety and were in charge of keeping up to date on new legislation that affected the company and the employees.

Later, the government stepped into the Human Resource field by adopting laws that regulated the work day, pay and child labor. During the Great Depression, these laws seemed no longer useful as it was difficult to find jobs. Although work was created by the government, there was not enough to go around. This led to the creation of pensions and other social programs. With many workers to fill each job, companies could afford to be more selective in their hiring.

The Norris-LaGuardia Act changed the political landscape by making "yellow-dog" contracts (a promise from an employee that they would not join a union) unenforceable. In 1935, The National Labor Relations Act (NLRA) also known as the Wagner Act helped unions become more powerful than ever. The Landrum-Griffith Act of 1959 is what protects union members if their leaders do anything illegal or are personally sued. We'll cover unions in depth later in the text.

Companies still believed that the way to keep employees was to boost productivity. Over the years they have added benefits such as:

- Health Insurance
- Sick Days
- Dental Insurance
- Vacation Pay
- 401k
- Tuition Reimbursement

Human Resources Functions

HR Managers work together with managers of other departments to achieve several objectives. HR Managers:

- Counsel and give advice to employees and their managers on various issues. They help develop and implement policies and rules that meet the company's objectives. For example, if a company wants to reduce the amount of money it spends on temporary workers, it could find a way to reduce the number of days an employee calls in sick. HR managers have the experience to design programs that will get the employees into work each and every day.

- HR managers perform many administrative functions such as hiring, firing, training, testing, and handling HR-related complaints. There are new terms used to describe the HR management tasks. Selection means hiring, as in "selecting" a new employee. Termination means "firing" an employee. Lay-offs, riffs, downsizing all mean a "reduction in force," which is a fancy way of saying you will be leaving many people without jobs. Employee development means the same as employee training.

- HR Managers also work with the Executive level of the company to create policies and to implement those policies. HR managers can help determine the specifics about the way a policy is implemented. For example, they may decide that clocking in one minute after the time the employee is due to be present to work is acceptable, but three minutes means that employee is late and will be reprimanded.

- HR managers also function as an advocate of employees. When an employee has a complaint, such as a sexual harassment issue, they can approach the HR management to get assistance in correcting the situation.

Motivation

William James of Harvard University conducted research on Motivation. His findings are noteworthy. He found that hourly employees whose work pattern he studied could hold on to their jobs if they performed at 20 to 30% of their ability. His studies further elucidated that workmen can work up to 80 to 90% of their ability if they are highly motivated! In other words if the employees are highly motivated their work ability jumps from 20-30% to 80-90%!

For some, money can be a good motivator. For others, safety, i.e., security, job-satisfaction, congenial atmosphere, social needs, esteem needs and self-actualization needs are important. Challenge in one's job is a motivation for some people. Rewards for accomplishments are also a motivator.

Hawthorne Effect

In 1927 a series of studies began at Western Electric Company in Hawthorne, Illinois. The first study was testing the assumption that the worker output would increase if the level of light in the plant was turned up. To test the theory, they took several female workers into a separate room in the factory and tested their output against a variety of lighting. Surprisingly, output increased regardless of the light level, until it was too dark to see and remained constant. Why? By taking the workers into another room at the plant, they had done something inadvertently; they had made the workers feel special. Experts coin this example to be the Hawthorne effect, which is where an interest in the organization's people's problems effect the output, not the changes themselves.

Leadership

Peter F. Drucker, the Modern Management philosopher and guru, states in his book, "The Practice of Management," "...The successful organization has one major attribute that sets it apart from unsuccessful organizations: dynamic and effective leadership...." Again, George R Terry, in his wonderful book "Principles of Management" points out that: "...Of every one hundred new business establishments started, approximately fifty, or one half, go out of business within two years. By the end of five years, only one third of the original one hundred will still be in business...." Almost all the failures were attributed to ineffective leadership. This tells us in clear and unambiguous terms all about leadership. In other words, the core of leadership is accomplishment of goals with and through people. Every leader has a style. The style of leaders is the consistent behavior patterns that they exhibit when they seek to influence people in order to accomplish organizational goals. The style is the consistent perception of the followers/subordinates of the leader.

There are despotic leaders who only demand what they want normally in high decibels, and encourage no initiative. They are task leaders. On the other side of the spectrum you have leaders who value human relationships, who are polite but firm with subordinates, encourage initiative and are willing to share responsibilities.

Many leaders empower their employees by allowing them to make their own decisions and/or giving them authorization for employing specific behaviors to help customers.

Theory X & Y

Theory X is a management approach where you believe that people dislike work and responsibility and are only motivated by money and other financial incentives. It also assumes that these people must be micro managed and supervised.

Theory Y is the assumption that where you believe that all people enjoy work, and will control their own performance if you give them the chance. These people will want to do a good job and work better with a hands off approach.

Communication

In communication there is a sender and a receiver. If the sender sends information (message) to the receiver and if the information is understood in full by the receiver, you have communicated successfully. The main purpose of communication in an organizational setting is to influence action aimed at achieving the common goals of the organization.

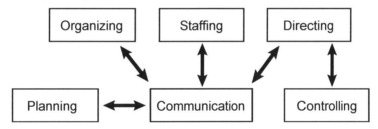

Communication is a very important factor in effective leadership and management. Not only the leaders (superiors) but also the followers (subordinates) should be adept in communicating.

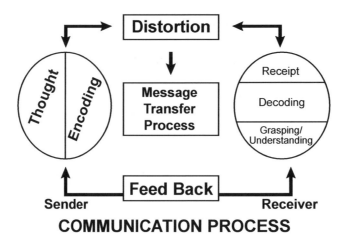

COMMUNICATION PROCESS

In an organization there are upward and downward communication, horizontal communication and diagonal communication.

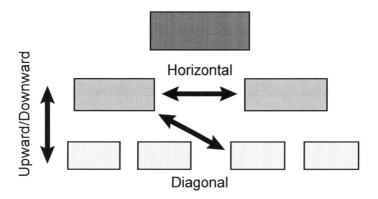

Communication can be oral, written or non-verbal. When a message is repeated through various media, the comprehension and recall of that message is high with the receiver of such message. Simple words, using personal pronouns, adding graphs or graphics, short sentenced paragraphs, logical, cohesive and cogent presentation, and avoiding verborrhea will ensure good communication.

🎓 *Delphi Technique*

The Delphi method (also the Delphi technique) was developed by RAND, the Santa Monica, California, "think tank" in the 1950s as a group communication process. The method is designed to achieve a convergence of opinion on a particular real-world topic through detailed examination and discussion. The Delphi method is a long process of asking questions and gathering feedback. Participants often include experts on the topic. The result of using the Delphi method successfully is a majority group opinion. Delphi theory is predicated on the value of a single expert group opinion. The Delphi method has been adopted for science and technology forecasting, policy-making, policy investigation, and goal-setting.

The process of the Delphi method occurs as follows: A facilitator sends out question-naires to select individuals which pertain to a particular topic. A group of participants respond to the questionnaires. The participants represent a wide range of opinions and expertise on the topic. When completed, the responses from the participants are returned to the facilitator to process the information. They often identify the main common and conflicting viewpoints represented by the participants. The answers of the group are returned to the participants in the form of a statistical representation of the group response, along with another questionnaire and any other pertinent information. The process can repeated as many times as necessary. The process has succeeded when the range of responses have reduced and the participants have arrived at a consensus. The key design characteristics of the Delphi method eliminate many of the usual prob-lems of group discussion. The facilitator controls all interaction among the participants, so all participants are anonymous. Because the participants remain anonymous, they can answer honestly and can change their position without fear of judgment. Personal bias, personality, and reputation cannot influence their decision. The participants can change their position at any time. The main value of the Delphi technique lies in the ideas that are created. Though the goal is to obtain a single expert opinion, the new ideas and differing opinions that often form are also valuable.

Ethical Aspects of Decision Making

Ethics in HRM is an important factor. HR managers are expected to know and imple-ment all the legal issues that come with running an organization. But sometimes, what is the law and what is right are not in line. Most large corporations have an ethical code, mission statement or value statement. The HR manager helps implement these statements of culture. A company may be complying with a federal program to hire minorities but it is up to the managers and the HR managers to ensure that these em-ployees, once hired, are treated equally to other employees. A simple way to describe this is: HR managers need to "walk the walk" as well as "talk the talk." HR managers must make policies congruent with mission statements.

Human Resource Planning

HR Managers have a great deal of desk work to do. In fact, that is the majority of their work. They must create and implement new policies, procedures, plans, parties, etc., for the organization. They are in charge of personnel and job design.

Job Analysis & Job Design

Many of you may not be familiar with job analysis and job design. Most small-to-medium size companies do not take the time to write out job descriptions and other related policies. In fact, they may not even have a completely dedicated person to perform HR management. The person who does the payroll accounts sometimes falls into this catchall position.

In large corporations, many people spend all day every day doing tasks that you didn't know existed and didn't know were important. One of these tasks is job analysis. Job analysis is a specific, scientific way of categorizing exactly what skills and tasks a specific job requires. Job analysis is a way to justify a job description, which is not the same thing. To create a job analysis, you must discover what job tasks or activities these jobs require. For example, a job analysis for an administrative assistant may include:

- Write and answer e-mails
- Schedule meetings
- Fax documents
- Copy memos
- Order catering
- Schedule travel
- Schedule interviews
- Order supplies

Job analysis is the actual requirements and tasks of a job. Job design is different. Job design is the ideal traits for a position. Taking our example of an administrative assistant, job design would be as follows:

- Self-starting person
- Works well under pressure
- Knowledgeable about computers
- Familiar with office machines
- Able to negotiate pricing

Do you see the difference? Maybe you have seen a job posting with actual skills (job analysis) and one with ideal traits (job design).

The reason that job analysis so important and needs to be done correctly is that it also has legal implications. You must show job relatedness of a particular position. For example, you cannot say "the administrative assistant must have blonde hair" because you do not have a job analysis function that is linked to it. Now that example may be extreme so here is one more likely. An administrative assistant who works for a general contractor may have "shelf inventory" as one of the items listed in their job analysis. If an individual was unable to perform that task through a disability, the company would be legally protected if that person sued for discrimination. So in summary, you can't hire or fire based on issues that are not directly related to the job.

The ADA, Americans with Disabilities Act, requires that job duties (which make up your job analysis) must be essential functions for success in that job. If the job requires certain tasks, such as driving, climbing and lifting, then those requirements must be stated in the job description.

The three items that make an essential function are:

- The position is there to allow performance of the function
- There are no other people in the organization that can perform that function reasonably
- The function is highly specialized or requires special training

There are so many terms in this section so here is a recap of the terms we just learned.

Job analysis: the process of making a list of the exact tasks or activities that an individual in a specific job does

Job design: the ideal requirements of a job or person

Job description: a listing of what a job includes such as tasks, duties and responsibilities (analysis is the process of creating a job description)

Job relatedness: how essential job tasks are related to the job

The Hay Plan

The hay plan is used for job evaluation. Named for its creator, the Hay group, the hay plan is based on:

- Know-how - knowledge possessed by the manager, however acquired

- Problem solving - how the manager performs by creating solutions to problems

- Accountability - how the manager is accountable to the company through their performance

Personnel Administration

All resources in an organization need management, i.e., they are subjected to the processes of management viz., planning, organizing, directing and controlling. Buildings and machinery are physical resources. Stocks, bank balances are financial resources. People are human resources. While no other resource – capital, land, machines - can talk back, only human resources can think and talk back and this makes management of this resource that much more difficult.

Personnel Administration is that branch of general management which: (a) looks into manpower resources of an organization (b) has a managerial function of planning, organizing, directing and controlling and an operative function of recruiting, developing, compensating, integrating human resources together with keeping records on manpower (c) aims at harmonious labor (d) aims to achieve organizational goals by integrating human resources.

The term "industrial relations" is a broader concept, which seeks to bring in harmonious relationship between labor, management and the government of an industry.

Managing diversity is when you create a work environment where women, minorities and people with disabilities can perform and succeed on the job.

The term "labor management" normally defines the managing of manual workers of an organization. Working conditions and worker discipline together with the general recruitment, selection, compensation, etc., are dealt with by labor management.

The scope of "personnel management" is truly wider. It deals with the recruitment, selection, placement, training, compensation, working condition, and so on, pertaining to all categories of personnel in an organization. Personnel administration also deals with generation of mutual trust, total cooperation and cohesive workforce culture, and maintaining cordial relations with trade unions.

Affirmative action is a detailed plan that a company makes to recruit women and minorities into positions and promotions. The glass ceiling is a term used to describe the attitudes and unwritten policies that have blocked women or any person from moving up the corporate ladder.

Staffing

In organizing we have seen authority structures, broad departmentalization, delegation, etc. In other words we have a structure and we need people to fill up the structures to do meaningful jobs. Staffing, therefore, is a systematic and methodical filling up of positions in an organizational structure by identifying total manpower requirements, recruitment, selection, placement, appraisal, promotion, training and compensation. Organizing and staffing are closely linked.

Recruiting

There are many ways that a supervisor or manager can recruit talented employees, such as:

- Newspaper Ads
- Television Ads
- Workforce Services (administered by the state)
- Headhunters
- Staffing Firms
- Word of Mouth
- College Recruitment
- Competitor Recruitment
- Company's Website

Some of these resources for recruiting are internal and some are external. Internal sources would include promoting from within current employees. External is hiring any candidate from outside the company. Recruiting is the process of getting highly qualified individuals interested in the positions that you have available. Many organizations choose to recruit from within their own ranks. This can be beneficial to morale and show a pattern of success to other employees. Headhunters are groups of people that locate and place talented people in open jobs. If you hire through a headhunter, generally you are paying a premium which could be 30 to 40% of the new hire's salary. This makes using headhunter or executive search firms not as attractive as other methods but they can be valuable when looking to fill special or highly technical jobs.

Selection

Once an HR manager has a qualified pool of applicants, he or she will begin conducting interviews. Selection is taking that pool of applicants and narrowing it down to only the best. This is where job analysis comes in. Because you have determined that you need a specific group of skills called a skill set, you can determine which candidates will be the best at performing those skills or skill set.

Some jobs will require testing. This could include typing tests, computer testing or other skills. These tests can be done inside the organization or can be conducted through workforce services, a state agency, which will certify the results. They can also be administered in house (by the company). For example, Payless Shoes gives a simple written honesty test which asks potential employees about different situations. Based on their scores, some candidates are not eligible for hiring. Since implementing this screening process, Payless Shoes has reduced employee theft by 20%. Nordstrom uses a popular honesty test called the Reid Survey which helps screen out potentially dishonest employees.

There are two kinds of tests. An aptitude test measures a new hire's potential. An achievement test measures what a person already knows. KSAO is a term used to stand for a person's knowledge, skills, abilities and other characteristics. Selection tests must be standardized (the same every time), objective (not intended to discriminate), be valid (measure what they say they measure, like honesty), and have norms (normal scores and predictable patterns).

Graphology is another type of test that can be administered. Graphology is a scientific analysis of your handwriting. Generally, this is only done by organizations such as the CIA or FBI. Most regard it with skepticism of its validity but it is still administered. Personality tests can also be required.

A polygraph or lie-detector test is generally not given. The Employee Polygraph Protection Act of 1988 prohibits the use of polygraph in pre-hire screening except in the case of government agencies, pharmaceutical companies, and security guards.

Some companies will also require a drug test. These types of tests are almost always contracted out to a local facility which will send the results directly to the company. Sometimes a physical examination will be required. Reference checks are different from background checks. Reference checks are used to confirm items such as employment dates and education levels.

The steps to hiring an individual can be as follows. Keep in mind that some companies vary their steps based on their corporate policy.

1. New applicant submits application – initial screening
2. Resumes are reviewed and several individuals are selected for interviews
3. Testing of skills takes place
4. Interviews are conducted either alone or in teams
5. Decision to hire is made
6. Background check is completed on potential new employee
7. Drug test completed
8. New hire offer/letter signed and mailed

Now that you know the stages of the process, we will go into one of the major steps in detail, interviewing.

Interviewing

Conducting an interview is an important part of hiring a new person for your company. A group interview is where several applicants meet with one or more company representative. A board or team interview is when only one applicant meets with several company employees at one time.

It is best to have a list of questions prepared to ask all the people that you are interviewing. Because past performance is the best indicator of future performance, it is important to ask a candidate about what types of projects or problems they have worked with in the past.

For example, if you are hiring for a high stress job, after certain needs are met, such as education and experience, you will want to ask about other stressful situations they have had and how they dealt with them. If you are hiring them to manage a team, you will want to know about experiences where they have managed themselves, a team, their timelines and other related projects.

Interviewing is very important but you must also be very careful. There are laws to protect prospective employees in protected classes. You may not ask the applicants:

- Age
- Race
- Marital Status
- Religion
- Familial Status (questions about existing children)
- Disabilities

You may also not ask any questions that would lead you to any of those answers such as "What year did you graduate high school?" or anything similar. This would violate EEO laws.

The Big Five

The Big Five is the most widely used and accepted model of personality. It refers to five main personality types including agreeableness, conscientiousness, extroversion, neuroticism, and openness. The acronyms OCEAN and CANOE both represent the five personality traits. It is commonly used in the workplace and in creating effective teams. An employer can use the assessment to determine the traits that a potential employee has that are useful to them, that suit the needs of the job, and that work well with the other employees. Teams with similar personality profiles based on the big five tend to work well together.

The personality types are assessed by taking a test with questions that relate to one or more of the Big Five. The test for the personality types typically contains questions such as "I am easily distracted," "I am a private person" or "I enjoy meeting new people" which are answered on a scale ranging from "strongly agree" to "strongly disagree." A person can test high, mid-range, or low in each individual trait. A very high or very low score in a trait represents a strong personality indicator, and a mid-range score represents being neutral or average. For example, a high score in extroversion indicates an outgoing and energetic person, a mid-range score indicates average social inclination, and a low score indicates solitary and reserved person. Each trait similarly ranges from two opposite personality types.

Descriptions of the Big Five traits are as follows:

Openness (inventive/curious vs. consistent/cautious)
Openness describes a person who is imaginative, insightful, curious, thinks out-of-the-box, and has a broad range of interests.

Conscientiousness (efficient/organized vs. easy-going/careless)
Conscientiousness describes a person who is thoughtful, goal-oriented, detail-oriented, organized, and self-disciplined.

Extraversion (outgoing/energetic vs. solitary/reserved)
Extraversion describes a person who is sociable, talkative, assertive, emotionally expressive, and energetic.

Agreeableness (friendly/compassionate vs. analytical/detached)
Agreeableness describes a person who is trusting, altruistic, kind, affectionate, compassionate, and cooperative.

Neuroticism (sensitive/nervous vs. secure/confident)
Neuroticism describes a person who is sensitive and easily expresses anxiety, anger, irritability, and sadness.

 # *Promotions and Transfers*

Sometimes when looking for a person to fill a new position, HR managers don't have to look very far. This means that the best employee for the job could already be within the organization. Sometimes promotions are based on employee seniority. Other times the company will choose the most qualified person, regardless of the amount of time they have been with the company. However, most companies use a blending of these policies. HR managers not only help select the individual, but they also create the policies about moving up. A promotion is different from a transfer. Generally, a transfer puts an employee in a new position but with a similar pay and responsibilities. Some companies use job/pay grades in order to standardize salaries and benefits. Transfers can be a way to motivate an employee with new challenges while keeping costs down for the company.

Layoffs

There are many names for layoffs which include: downsizing, riffs, reduction in force. All these terms are used to soften the blow to the employees and to the media when the decision is made to reduce the number of employees for whatever reason. Although these terms can be used interchangeably by the media, for our purposes there are a few differences in the terminology. A layoff can be a temporary or permanent termination of employment based on the company not having enough money to pay workers or because there is not any work to be done.

It does not have to be all workers but some that are affected in a layoff. In some settings, including a union-based setting, it is the least senior employees that leave first. However, that is not always the case. For example, a company looking to cut costs can layoff a sales person who has been there 12 years and makes $56,000 a year or they can layoff someone who has been there 2 years and makes $29,000. If both employees perform at the same rate, then it makes economic sense to terminate the more senior employee because the company will save the most. This type of action has sent employee loyalty into a tailspin as workers realize they are expendable.

Downsizing is a term used when the company wants to reduce its employees to improve the bottom line. This may be done to raise stock prices or reduce overhead to make the company more attractive to investors. Voluntary turnover is when employees are given the option to quit or take early retirement. This may be attractive to employees who had planned on leaving the company or the workforce altogether, and now have a financial incentive to do so.

When employees are terminated, they can be offered severance pay or a benefits package. Severance is a check for a certain amount of money, mainly based on your time with the company and or any vacation days that were unused as of the date of termination. Included with the benefits package can be assistance with outplacement, which is the process of helping an old employee find work at a new company.

 # Working with a Diverse Workforce

A supervisor's team has many different people. Each person brings their own unique problems, values, strengths and experiences to the team. A diverse workforce generally includes minorities, different genders and people with disabilities. It is important to remember that each employee cannot be motivated the same way. Cultures must also be considered when supervising. For example, a Hispanic worker may have different cultural holidays they celebrate with their family than another peer. Some employees may have problems working on Sunday because it interferes with their worship services or religious beliefs.

Multinational Corporations

A multinational corporation (MNC), also called an international corporation, is a corporation with facilities, factories, offices, assets, or transactions in at least one country other than its home country. It can also be a "transnational corporation" which also conducts business in multiple countries but does not claim a home country. Management of the company as a whole is usually coordinated from a main office or headquarters.

The subsidiaries report to the main office. The majority of large multinationals are American, Japanese or Western European. Examples of multinational corporations include McDonald's, Coca-Cola, Wal-Mart, Google, and many airlines, car companies, and banks.

Human resource management is important to maintaining good working relations, though some companies are more successful at this than others. Managing international human resources is more complex because of the many differences between the headquarters and the subsidiaries, such as culture and language. There tends to be more risk of discrimination based on religion, race, sex, social or economic class, and nationality. It is important for companies to actively maintain equality.

Human resource management is involved in staffing, training and development, performance appraisal, communication and labor relations. Staffing policies depend on a company's approach to globalization. Depending on the company's goal to either maintain the home country's standard as much as possible or adapt to the country, they may fill top management positions with home country nationals or local nationals. It's also important to identify and develop local talent, which can be done through Management Development Programs (MDP). These programs help improve the coordination between employees with diverse cultural, religious and educational backgrounds. Performance appraisal is another activity managed by subsidiary managers, who establish the criteria of measuring performance. Performance Management links performance appraisal to employee training, development, and compensation.

Those in management positions are largely responsible for maintaining good local position at subsidiaries. This can be difficult, especially when differences of opinion arise between headquarters and a subsidiary. Some subsidiaries are largely self-maintained, and some are heavily directed from headquarters. There are three theories concerning subsidiary's autonomy in decision-making. According to limited autonomy, the degree of autonomy depends on the MNC's approach to globalization. According to variable autonomy, the degree of autonomy varies with the degree of internationalization of the company. According to negotiated autonomy, the degree of autonomy of a subsidiary depends on its ability to negotiate with headquarters.

Employee Counseling

Employees are not perfect. They can have problems with attendance, morale, drugs, anger, alcohol, attitude or even problems just completing their duties. Many companies offer counseling for problems such as alcohol or drug addiction. Other companies offer the assistance of professional counselors, psychologists and psychiatrists through their medical coverage programs. Generally, employers will NOT pay for family or marriage counseling.

Training and Development

Training can be considered as a program built primarily to assist employee development. The smarter your employees are at doing their jobs, the more productive they will be. Training can teach them the basics of their current job or can teach them new skills to get a promotion or move to a different department. When a company wants to train their employees for future roles it is called employee development vs. employee training.

There are various kinds of training, which include:

- Apprenticeship
- Refresher courses
- Programmed learning – teaching job skills in a school-like format. The employee is taught information, asked questions, and reviews the answers with the trainer.
- Promotional training
- Job instruction training – a step-by-step method of teaching a job
- Vestibule training – training in an offsite facility that mimics the job environment
- On the job training – when you learn the job by actually doing it.
- Off the job training

The specific purposes behind training are:

- Knowledge and skill enhancement
- Making it possible to introduce new methods. Encouraging people to learn new methods makes it possible for the personnel to work more effectively and efficiently.
- Knowledge on safety. It provides the much needed knowledge on how to operate machines with less risk.
- Utilizing the latest techniques: Training impacts knowledge on the latest techniques available and makes the operator much more skilful and technique-oriented.
- Morale boosting: Promotes self-confidence of personnel as they are trained in skills, knowledge, aptitude and attitude necessary to do their job most efficiently.
- Self-actualization: It paves the way for employees to realize their full potential.

Many corporate business houses have substantial training budgets to augment and fine tune their managerial skills. On-the-job training for managers includes:

- Planned progression
- Temporary promotion

- Job rotation – employees are moved from one department to another in order to understand how the business works
- The committee method or junior board – employees sit on a board and review company problems and find solutions
- Coaching – the new employee works with the employee they are replacing

Off-the-job training may consist of:

- Coaching – from an external party
- Conference
- Group dynamics
- Idea tracking
- Managerial games – teams of managers compete in fictional companies with fictional problems for prizes
- Multimedia presentations
- Role playing – managers "pretend" to be in a certain role during training to help them understand both sides of a problem
- Programmed learning
- Organizational development – employees are taught the new corporate values, strategies to implement in their job functions
- Workshop
- Special tuition

Training is easier to learn and more enjoyable to the employee if they understand why they are learning the information and how it will be important in their future. This "buy-in" from employees makes the training seem more important and worth the employee's full attention and their time. Motivation is critical with training. In a perfect training environment, employees should be able to pace themselves until the task is mastered. Praise to new employees helps them feel better about their new skills and makes them more confident.

Training should be broken up into modules or chunks of information. A training program is the most successful if it gives the employees the time to practice and train in a similar setting to the one they will be working in. For example, a training room for a call center would have the same layout. Each desk would have a computer and a phone. The employees would be able to practice taking calls as a group. For example, a trainer would be the caller and each employee in the training room would be able to follow along on his or her monitor as if it was a real call.

Performance Appraisals

An organization's current human resources need timely evaluation of their capabilities in order to be ready for any future needs. There are two sources where managers look to appraise capabilities of human resources. The first is personnel records (which are built on the applications submitted) and second, personnel appraisal ratings.

Personnel records give all the data in the application together with high school, college and other educational institutional records, selection test scores, salary/wage started and changes made during the service, promotional opportunities availed, transfer effected, training courses attended, disciplinary actions, if any, recorded and personnel appraisal ratings.

The main purpose of any personnel appraisal plan is to help the employee to know his strengths and weaknesses, opportunities and threats (SWOT) and in order to build in him the ability to meet ever increasing job challenges. Constructive criticism and helpful dialogue are excellent guidance for the employee to gain perspective and mental maturity to perform his allotted tasks skillfully and rise on the organization ladder. Companies rate many items pertaining to an individual and we give below an excerpt which illustrates this concept.

Most companies have their own appraisal methods but the data normally sought to rate belongs to any one of the elements given above.

Good companies normally rate the person on the basis of his job-performance, attitude and behavior.

Performance appraisals, quarterly reviews or performance evaluations are all the same thing. They are usually handled by the employee's immediate supervisor, sometimes with the help of the HR manager. The HR department trains managers on how to give performance appraisals that are beneficial to both the employee and to the company.

The main purposes of performance appraisals are:

- Getting information to make decisions about raises, bonuses and promotions
- Reviewing employee behavior (and correcting if necessary)
- Talking about career planning and long term goals

There are many methods of job evaluation or performance appraisal techniques.

- Ranking system: In this jobs are ranked on the basis of responsibilities and duties and their importance to overall company objectives. Salary/wages are determined accordingly.

- Graphic rating scale method: rating employees on a list of traits or job requirements.

- Alternation ranking method: rating employees as a group from best to worst on a particular area.

- Paired comparison method: comparing each employee to every other employee in a particular area.

- Behaviorally anchored rating scales: matching ratings with employee behavior.

- Narrative forms: determining performance based on a written example of past behavior and future plans

- Critical incident method: keeping a record of an employee's positive or negative behavior.

- Management by objectives: employees are judged by specific goals and if they met their goals.

- Classification method: Grades are defined by the requirements found to be common to several tasks spanning different departments.

- Points system: Requirements appropriate to each job are analyzed and quantified. Job requirements are subdivided into smaller degrees and each degree is assigned points. The total points a job gets determines its relative position vis-à-vis the job structure.

- Factor Comparison: For a few predetermined key jobs, points are allotted and wage rates for such key jobs are fixed.

- Forced distribution method: Grouping employees in specific groups and grading their efforts on the curve.

All these methods can be divided into two categories, qualitative and quantitative. Qualitative is something that cannot be described numerically or put into a comparable format. Quantitative is anything that can be defined with numbers. For example, on his review John scored a five in customer satisfaction. Because the survey format was numerical it is quantitative. If it had been an open response survey and the customer had rated him as "helpful" that would be a qualitative statement.

A manager must be objective in the performance appraisal process. The halo effect can occur, which is when a supervisor skews their focus on all the employees traits based on a very good or very bad existing trait. For example, if you know that someone has a high IQ, you expect different behavior from them vs. from someone you don't know anything about. Central tendency is when anyone rates someone as "average" in all areas. Many people do this on written questionnaires or surveys but as a manager it is important NOT to do this so that the employee can improve. Bias is anything a supervisor may have against or for an employee. It means that the employee might be treated better because of their gender or treated worse because of their race. A manager must also be careful to not have bias towards any of their employees.

Discipline

Sometimes discipline is required to get employees back on the right track. Some government agencies and private businesses have strict rules and clearly defined consequences for breaking them. For example, many firms use a similar system comprised of:

- Verbal warnings
- Written warnings
- Suspension
- Termination

Other areas of industry such as call centers use a different approach. For example, each time an employee clocks in late or leaves work early, they are given ½ a point on their attendance. For a day they call in sick for work, they receive 1 full point. When an employee reaches 4 points in a six-month time frame, they are required to fill out an attendance contract with their supervisor. If an employee reaches 6 points, they are subject to termination.

Many states have what they call "at will" employees, which means that these employees may be fired at any time for any reason (except for Title VII infractions which include race, age, etc.). However, some businesses, in particular the government, have their policies so strict that they actually reduce the effectiveness of the supervisor. With some positions, so much documentation is required to terminate an employee it is almost impossible. They are required to receive a certain amount of warnings and suspensions before termination is even on the table. This is where the stereotype of a cushy "government" job got its start.

Another style of discipline is referred to as the **hot stove rule**. Just as there is an immediate response and reaction to touching a hot stove, so should there be in disciplining employees. There is also heat that comes from the stove, serving as a preliminary warning that it is hot. Also, a hot stove is always hot. Using consistent discipline offers better results.

Total Quality Management (TQM)

Quality of a product determines its salability. Products enjoying exceptional quality standards demand a premium. There should be a conscious effort to maintain a high quality in not only the end product, but even the methods, systems, communication and thinking of top level to the floor level employee. A good quality program includes:

- Determination of standards of quality
- Institution of an effective continuous on the job checking program with responsibilities and accountability firmly fixed
- A recording system for comparing errors vs. standards
- A method which spells out corrective action, and
- To install a program of analysis and quality improvement whenever found needed.

Checking on the production line while the job is on is a good system. However, it may not be possible to check every piece produced. Here the statistical quality methods come to help. Normally checking is done on a random basis (Random Sampling Method). The most common program liked by organizations is the acceptance sampling method. A sample, normally 10 to 15% of a batch from a running production line, is checked. If they find that a high majority of the checked batch quantities consistently match the set standards for qualitative accuracy, the entire batch (the balance of 90 to 85% as the case may be) is accepted. This is acceptance sampling in essence.

Today there is ISO-9000 (which tells us that a well thought out system will produce predicted quality consistently, with consistency in the implementation of the system at every stage – not only in design or production but in policies and actions of all employees), TQM – Total Quality Management (which tells us to continuously meet agreed customer requirements at the lowest cost, by realizing the potential of employees).

Six Sigma

Six Sigma is a finite, controlled, measured plan that a company adheres to in order to be as perfect as possible, with as little defects, returns, etc., as possible. This six comes from their methodology, no more than six standard deviations from the mean (average) of a statistic to their end result. What does that really mean? It means that when a product is rated six sigma, the product exhibits no more than 3.4 non conformities (defects) per million opportunities (NPMO) at the part and process levels. The methodology is broken down into two sub-methodologies the DMAIC and DMADV. The Six

Sigma DMAIC process stands for define, measure, analyze, improve, and control. This is used to improve existing policies and procedures.

The Six Sigma DMADV stands for define, measure, analyze, design, and verify. This set is used to develop a brand new product or procedure.
All these concepts aim to give a zero-defect product.

The quality movement has acquired many gurus. Chief among them are: (1) Phillip B. Crosby – who always emphasized "zero-defect," (2) Dr W. Edwards Deming – who is considered the forefather of Japanese quality revolution and the thrust of his philosophy has always been planned reduction of variation, and (3) Dr. Joseph Juran who always thought and taught that quality is achievable through people rather than technique.

Quality Circle

A quality circle is a group of volunteers who work in a related area that meet regularly on company time to solve problems and generate improvement in the workplace. The groups are usually small and include a supervisor or chairman. The main objectives during a meeting are to identify problems and to create solutions. Quality Circle groups generally address issues such as safety, product design, and manufacturing processes. Employees who participate in quality circles usually receive training in formal problem-solving methods to apply to specific or general company problems.

Wage and Salary Administration

Compensation is whatever money employees are paid to perform a task or function. Employees can be paid by the hour, by the piece or be salaried. Compensation also includes anything they receive such as bonuses, paid time off, vacation, 401k, etc.

A common problem for employers is establishing fair wages across the board. This can be a major internal problem when a more tenured employee discovers they are earning less than a new hire. To establish pay rates in the corporate world, there are several steps to make this a more structured process. The more processes you have, the less likelihood of having legal problems in the future based on pay.

First, you may begin with a salary survey to determine what the going rate is for a specific job. We'll use the example of a secretary. To find out, you can contact employment agencies, look online and in the newspaper. We use these numbers as a benchmark. The process is then repeated for other major jobs in the organization.

Each job is then evaluated by compensable factors including:

- Responsibility
- Experience
- Skills
- Working conditions

These are used to show how much more or less is required from job to job. The easiest way to rank jobs is to use categories, classes and grades. Each pay grade is a certain number. For example, grade 6 will equate to $24,000 per year. Grade 22 will equate to $42,000 per year. You can then assign particular grades to certain job functions.

Rate ranges give you a way to pay employees in the same job title different amounts. All may be account managers but some may have more experience. Pay rates can be created based on the information from pay grades. Plot the salaries from each pay grade and using an arc line, plot your data. These can be your target wages.

However, keep in mind that this is a relatively old process for determining pay rates and is not used as much today as in the past. The most popular form of compensation is based on performance for the company.

Wages are sometimes developed by HR managers based on the market. There are three different levels that a company can base its pay on:

- Trailing the market
- Meeting the market
- Leading the market

An organization that is trailing the market is not paying as well as what the wages generally are in that geographic location and/or industry. These companies realize that they pay a lower wage, but have chosen to do so intentionally.

For example, a new programmer would work for less money at a large company like Google because they want the prestige of having that company on their resume. The individual and the company are taking a risk on each other. The company is hoping to get qualified talent for less, the employee is hoping to get an added benefit down the road of networking, stock price, prestige, etc.

When a company is meeting the market, they are paying what the local market demands for that position, no more and no less.

A company that is leading the market is paying more than the average wage in a particular sector. A company opening up in a new area may need to hire talent very quickly, and will lead the market in order to get those employees in a timely manner.

 Wages

Workweek - A workweek is a period of 168 hours during 7 consecutive 24-hour periods. It may begin on any day of the week and at any hour of the day established by the employer. Generally, for purposes of minimum wage and overtime payment, each workweek stands alone; there can be no averaging of 2 or more workweeks. Employee coverage, compliance with wage payment requirements, and the application of most exemptions are determined on a workweek basis.

Hours worked - Covered employees must be paid for all hours worked in a workweek. In general, "hours worked" includes all time an employee must be on duty, or on the employer's premises or at any other prescribed place of work. Also included is any additional time the employee is allowed (i.e., suffered or permitted) to work.

Overtime must be paid at a rate of at least one and one-half times the employee's regular rate of pay for each hour worked in a workweek in excess of the maximum allowable in a given type of employment. Generally, the regular rate includes all payments made by the employer to or on behalf of the employee (except for certain statutory exclusions). The following examples are based on a maximum 40-hour workweek.

Hourly rate (regular pay rate for an employee paid by the hour) - If more than 40 hours are worked, at least one and one-half times the regular rate for each hour over 40 is due.

Example: An employee paid $8.00 an hour works 44 hours in a workweek. The employee is entitled to at least one and one-half times $8.00, or $12.00, for each hour over 40. Pay for the week would be $320 for the first 40 hours, plus $48.00 for the four hours of overtime - a total of $368.00.

Piece rate - The regular rate of pay for an employee paid on a piecework basis is obtained by dividing the total weekly earnings by the total number of hours worked in that week. The employee is entitled to an additional one-half times this regular rate for each hour over 40, plus the full piecework earnings.

Example: An employee paid on a piecework basis works 45 hours in a week and earns $315. The regular rate of pay for that week is $315 divided by 45, or $7.00 an hour. In addition to the straight-time pay, the employee is also entitled to $3.50 (half the regular rate) for each hour over 40 - an additional $17.50 for the 5 overtime hours - for a total of $332.50.

Another way to compensate pieceworkers for overtime, if agreed to before the work is performed, is to pay one and one-half times the piece rate for each piece produced during the overtime hours. The piece rate must be the one actually paid during non-overtime hours and must be enough to yield at least the minimum wage per hour.

Commission - This is when employees are paid rewards based on a percentage of their sales. When an employee is paid salary and commission it is called a combination plan.

Salary - The regular rate for an employee paid a salary for a regular or specified number of hours a week is obtained by dividing the salary by the number of hours for which the salary is intended to compensate.

If, under the employment agreement, a salary sufficient to meet the minimum wage requirement in every workweek is paid as straight time for whatever number of hours is worked in a workweek, the regular rate is obtained by dividing the salary by the number of hours worked each week. To illustrate, suppose an employee's hours of work vary each week and the agreement with the employer is that the employee will be paid $420 a week for whatever number of hours of work is required. Under this agreement, the regular rate will vary in overtime weeks. If the employee works 50 hours, the regular rate is $8.40 ($420 divided by 50 hours). In addition to the salary, half the regular rate, or $4.20, is due for each of the 10 overtime hours, for a total of $462 for the week. If the employee works 60 hours, the regular rate is $7.00 ($420 divided by 60 hours). In that case, an additional $3.50 is due for each of the 20 overtime hours for a total of $490 for the week.

In no case may the regular rate be less than the minimum wage required by FLSA.

If a salary is paid on other than a weekly basis, the weekly pay must be determined in order to compute the regular rate and overtime pay. If the salary is for a half month, it must be multiplied by 24 and the product divided by 52 weeks to get the weekly equivalent. A monthly salary should be multiplied by 12 and the product divided by 52.

Red circle wages - When a worker is receiving a wage higher than the maximum salary for a position based on your employee compensation policy or current industry rates. Let's say that John was hired four years ago to put widgets in boxes. Every year John receives a raise so now he is making four dollars more an hour than when he first started. Each other employee in his department is at the initial pay rate. Your company determines that it will pay between $9-13 per hour for that position. Because John is already at that rate, his wage will be "circled" in red by management and a freeze will be put on further wage increases.

Incentive Plans

When your performance is directly linked to how much you get paid, it is called an incentive plan. There are different applications for each type of incentive plan. For example, a seamstress paid on a piecework plan will be paid depending on how many shirts or pockets that she sews. Each may only be worth as little as 75 cents but because she can sew 13-15 an hour she makes a good wage. The better and faster she can sew, the more money she will receive. Another type of incentive plan is called standard hour plan. A good example of this type of position is a telephone interviewer, someone who conducts telephone surveys. He or she will receive an hourly wage and an extra bonus for each survey completed. Sometimes teams are on an incentive plan where everyone is rewarded or penalized for the team's performance.

For higher positions such as managers and executive level positions, the incentive plans are more diverse. They include receiving stock options, which is the right to purchase (sometimes at a discount from the public) the company's stock in the future at the price it is today. This is valuable to the employee if the stock today is $4 a share and when they exercise their option (which means to buy and then sell the stock) they will be able to sell it for a higher amount, such as $30, resulting in a $26 profit. However, if the company fares poorly, this intangible reward loses its value. Some employees also receive an annual bonus based on meeting objectives and goals.

Some companies also participate in an ESOP plan. Employee stock ownership plan is when the employer gives the stock to the employee and they receive ownership of it at retirement or when they are fired or quit. This is what fueled several financial scandals in the last few years. Employees counted on the sale of the stock for retirement but the company went bankrupt, eroding the price of the stock. The values went from $60,000 to zero. Those employees were left "holding the bag" as they had not diversified their funds for retirement.

A gainsharing plan is when employees share in the "fruits of the labor" or basically, when the company does well or better than expected, each employee gets a bonus proportionate to their position and the degree of the company's success. On the flip-side, an at-risk pay plan puts a percentage of the employee's wage at risk which can be lost if the company does not do well. This is not a common practice for companies today.

Wage Garnishment

Wage garnishment is a legal procedure in which a person's earnings are required by court order to be withheld by an employer for the payment of a debt such as child support. Title III of the Consumer Credit Protection Act (CCPA) prohibits an employer from discharging an employee whose earnings have been subject to garnishment for any one debt, regardless of the number of levies made or proceedings brought to collect it.

Title III protects employees from being discharged by their employers because their wages have been garnished for any one debt and limits the amount of employees' earnings that may be garnished in any one week. It does not, however, protect an employee from discharge if the employee's earnings have been subject to garnishment for a second or subsequent debts.

Title III applies to all individuals who receive personal earnings and to their employers. Personal earnings include wages, salaries, commissions, bonuses, and income from a pension or retirement program, but do not ordinarily include tips.

Piecework

Under the Fair Labor Standards Act (FLSA), industrial homework (also called "piecework") means the production by any covered person in a home, apartment, or room in a residential establishment, of goods for an employer who permits or authorizes such production, regardless of the source (whether obtained from an employer or elsewhere) of the materials used by the home worker in producing these items.

The performance of certain types of industrial homework is prohibited under the FLSA unless the employer has obtained prior certification from the Department of Labor. Restrictions apply in the manufacture of knitted outerwear, gloves and mittens, buttons and buckles, handkerchiefs, embroideries, and jewelry, if there are no safety and health hazards. The manufacture of women's apparel (and jewelry under hazardous conditions) is generally prohibited. All individually covered homework is subject to the FLSA's minimum wage, overtime, and recordkeeping requirements. Employers must provide workers with handbooks to record time, expenses, and pay information.

Benefits

Benefits from corporations can be either financial and or non-financial. Financial benefits include:

- Paid vacation
- Paid sick days
- Paid bereavement days
- Paid holidays
- Severance pay
- Health insurance
- Dental insurance
- Vision insurance
- AD&D insurance
- 401k
- Education reimbursement
- Health club memberships
- Retirement plans
- Mental health insurance

Non financial benefits can include:

- Onsite day care
- Flextime (when employees can choose their own schedule, sometimes around a core period of hours, such as 10-2, but pick their own start and stop times)
- Four-day workweek (employees work four 10-hour days)
- Job sharing (when two or more people share a job or job responsibilities)
- Legal access
- Telecommuting (when an employee works from home some or all of the time)
- Flexyears (employees choose the hours they want to work for the next year based on months)
- Onsite cafeteria
- Onsite banking
- Onsite dry-cleaning
- Onsite shipping
- Onsite employee health club

For insurance, some companies use a cafeteria plan. This means you select only the insurance services you want. If you do not need vision insurance, you will not have to pay for it, or you can use that money for something else. Generally, the company gives each employee a certain amount per month to spend on insurance with the employee paying the rest of the amount from their paycheck.

Some states have requirements about what type of health care insurance is required to be provided to employees. Some rules are only for large companies with full time workers.

Termination

When an employee is terminated (dismissed) it is generally for one of the four following areas:

- Poor job performance, not being on time, calling in sick too many times, etc.
- Breaking company policies and rules
- Proving to be unqualified
- Unable to complete the job/tasks because the job has changed

Employment Law & Legal Issues

Risk management is an important area for supervisors. There are four ways to deal with risk:

1. Assuming the risk – setting aside enough money to pay for potential losses
2. Minimizing the risk – screening employees, utilizing network passwords, etc.
3. Avoiding the risk – avoiding certain industries (i.e., lumberjacking)
4. Shifting the risk – purchasing insurance policies

Many companies have goals regarding the number of accidents they are "allowed" to have in a certain period of time. Supervisors are awarded recognition and bonuses for having their team accident free.

Mediation and Arbitration

Mediation can be used when two parties cannot come to an agreement. Mediators are always a neutral third party, one that has no benefit or nothing to gain from the outcomes of the proceeding. Mediation is common in divorce and other legal matters where the two parties need a "voice of reason" to help guide negotiations and come to an acceptable resolution for both parties. What the mediators suggests and does is not legally binding but more of a informed counselor or friend that helps two parties to work things out. Examples include labor unions, private companies in dispute, parties in divorce, etc.

Arbitration differs from mediation on the following way - it is legally binding. Some courts will send cases to arbitration in order to clear the court docket or calendar for more pressing issues. While the arbitration is still a neutral third party, their decisions are legally binding.

In the fine print, many doctors and other companies require legal issues to go to arbitration to avoid costly courtroom battles.

 Taft Hartley Act

In 1947, Congress passed the Taft Hartley Act which outlawed for unions the closed shop, jurisdictional strikes, and secondary boycotts. It set up machinery for decertifying unions and allowed the states to pass more stringent legislation against unions such as right to work laws. Employers and unions were forbidden to contribute funds out of their treasuries to candidates for federal office, supervision was denied union protection, and the unions seeking the services of the National Labor Relations Board had to file their constitutions, by laws, and financial statements with the U.S. Department of Labor. Their officers also had to sign a non communist affidavit.

 *COBRA*

COBRA stands for The Comprehensive Omnibus Budget Reconciliation Act. It requires employers to allow employees to retain medical insurance after they quit or are terminated, for up to 18 months. It gives workers and their families who lose their health benefits the right to choose to continue group health benefits provided by their group health plan for limited periods of time under certain circumstances such as voluntary or involuntary job loss, reduction in the hours worked, transition between jobs, death, divorce, and other life events. Qualified individuals may be required to pay the entire premium for coverage up to 102 percent of the cost to the plan.

COBRA generally requires that group health plans sponsored by employers with 20 or more employees in the prior year offer employees and their families the opportunity for a temporary extension of health coverage (called continuation coverage) in certain instances where coverage under the plan would otherwise end.

COBRA outlines how employees and family members may elect continuation coverage. It also requires employers and plans to provide notice.

OSHA

OSHA stands for the Occupational Safety & Health Administration. OSHA's mission is to assure the safety and health of America's workers by setting and enforcing standards; providing training, outreach, and education; establishing partnerships; and encouraging continual improvement in workplace safety and health.

Nearly every working man and woman in the nation comes under OSHA's jurisdiction (with some exceptions such as miners, transportation workers, many public employees, and the self-employed). Other users and recipients of OSHA services include: occupational safety and health professionals, the academic community, lawyers, journalists, and personnel of other government entities.

The United States Department of Labor is in charge of making sure companies are in compliance with federal employment laws.

OSHA has four levels of priorities:

1. Inspect for immediately dangerous circumstances/locations
2. Research catastrophes, accidents or deaths involving five people or more
3. Investigate employee concerns about an unsafe working environment
4. Inspections for companies and industries with hazardous or high injury to health

OSHA provides certain documents to help administer policies and procedures. One of the most important is OSHA form 300, which is a log of work-related injuries and illnesses. These injuries and illnesses must be logged when they are directly related to the workplace. Conditions that must be logged include:

- Death
- Days away from work
- Medical treatment beyond first aid
- Loss of consciousness
- Restricted work activity or job transfer

 # EEO

EEO stands for Equal Employment Opportunity. This is a commission that investigates and prosecutes those business and individuals who discriminate against protected classes, such as discrimination involving:

- Age
- Disability
- Equal Pay
- National Origin
- Pregnancy
- Race
- Religion
- Retaliation
- Sex
- Sexual Harassment

 # Equal Pay Act of 1963

No employer having employees subject to any provisions of this section shall discriminate, within any establishment in which such employees are employed, between employees on the basis of sex by paying wages to employees in such establishment at a rate less than the rate at which he pays wages to employees of the opposite sex in such establishment for equal work on jobs the performance of which requires equal skill, effort, and responsibility, and which are performed under similar working conditions, except where such payment is made pursuant to (i) a seniority system; (ii) a merit system; (iii) a system which measures earnings by quantity or quality of production; or (iv) a differential based on any other factor other than sex, provided that an employer who is paying a wage rate differential in violation of this subsection shall not, in order to comply with the provisions of this subsection, reduce the wage rate of any employee. Another word for equal pay is comparable worth generally used in this same context. Comparable worth is the idea that men and women should be paid equal wages for doing comparable work. Some companies use a comparable worth point system (similar to a job grade) to equal out employee pay.

ERISA

The Employee Retirement Income Security Act of 1974 (ERISA) is a federal law that sets minimum standards for most voluntarily established pension and health plans in private industry to provide protection for individuals in these plans.

ERISA requires plans to provide participants with plan information including important information about plan features and funding; provides fiduciary responsibilities for those who manage and control plan assets; requires plans to establish a grievance and appeals process for participants to get benefits from their plans; and gives participants the right to sue for benefits and breaches of fiduciary duty.

There have been a number of amendments to ERISA, expanding the protections available to health benefit plan participants and beneficiaries. One important amendment, the Consolidated Omnibus Budget Reconciliation Act (COBRA), provides some workers and their families with the right to continue their health coverage for a limited time after certain events, such as the loss of a job.

Another amendment to ERISA is the Health Insurance Portability and Accountability Act (HIPAA), which provides important new protections for working Americans and their families who have preexisting medical conditions or might otherwise suffer discrimination in health coverage based on factors that relate to an individual's health. Other important amendments include the Newborns' and Mothers' Health Protection Act, the Mental Health Parity Act, and the Women's Health and Cancer Rights Act.

In general, ERISA does not cover group health plans established or maintained by governmental entities, churches for their employees, or plans which are maintained solely to comply with applicable workers compensation, unemployment, or disability laws. ERISA also does not cover plans maintained outside the United States primarily for the benefit of nonresident aliens or unfunded excess benefit plans.

ADA

Title I of the Americans with Disabilities Act (ADA) prohibits employers of 15 or more workers, employment agencies, and labor organizations of 15 or more workers from discriminating against qualified individuals with disabilities.

Title II of the Americans with Disabilities Act (ADA) prohibits state and local governments from discriminating against qualified individuals with disabilities in programs, activities, and services.

The Vietnam Era Veterans' Readjustment Assistance Act (VEVRAA) prohibits discrimination against and requires affirmative action for qualified special disabled veterans, as well as other categories of veterans. This law is enforced by the OFCCP.

Section 188 of the Workforce Investment Act of 1998 (WIA) prohibits discrimination against qualified individuals with disabilities who are applicants, employees, and participants in WIA Title I-financially assisted programs and activities, and programs that are part of the One-Stop system. Section 188 also prohibits discrimination on the grounds of age, race, color, religion, sex, national origin, political affiliation or belief, and for beneficiaries only, citizenship or participation in a WIA Title I-financially assisted program or activity. This law is enforced by the Civil Rights Center.

 **FMLA**

The Family and Medical Leave Act (FMLA) provides certain employees with up to 12 weeks of unpaid, job-protected leave per year. It also requires that their group health benefits be maintained during the leave.

FMLA is designed to help employees balance their work and family responsibilities by allowing them to take reasonable unpaid leave for certain family and medical reasons. It also seeks to accommodate the legitimate interests of employers and promote equal employment opportunity for men and women.

FMLA applies to all public agencies, all public and private elementary and secondary schools, and companies with 50 or more employees. These employers must provide an eligible employee with up to 12 weeks of unpaid leave each year for any of the following reasons:

- for the birth and care of the newborn child of an employee;
- for placement with the employee of a child for adoption or foster care;
- to care for an immediate family member (spouse, child, or parent) with a serious health condition; or
- to take medical leave when the employee is unable to work because of a serious health condition.

Employees are eligible for leave if they have worked for their employer at least 12 months, at least 1,250 hours over the past 12 months, and work at a location where the company employs 50 or more employees within 75 miles. Whether an employee has worked the minimum 1,250 hours of service is determined according to FLSA principles for determining compensable hours or work.

Time taken off work due to pregnancy complications can be counted against the 12 weeks of family and medical leave.

Special rules apply to employees of local education agencies. The Department of Labor administers FMLA; however, the Office of Personnel Management (OPM) administers FMLA for most federal employees.

 Age Discrimination

The Age Discrimination Act of 1975 prohibits discrimination on the basis of age in programs and activities receiving federal financial assistance. The Act, which applies to all ages, permits the use of certain age distinctions and factors other than age that meet the Act's requirements. The Age Discrimination Act is enforced by the Civil Rights Center.

The Age Discrimination in Employment Act of 1967 (ADEA) protects certain applicants and employees 40 years of age and older from discrimination on the basis of age in hiring, promotion, discharge, compensation, or terms, conditions or privileges of employment. The ADEA is enforced by the Equal Employment Opportunity Commission (EEOC).

Section 188 of the Workforce Investment Act of 1998 (WIA) prohibits discrimination against applicants, employees and participants in WIA Title I-financially assisted programs and activities, and programs that are part of the One-Stop system, on the ground of age. In addition, WIA prohibits discrimination on the grounds of race, color, religion, sex, national origin, disability, political affiliation or belief, and for beneficiaries only, citizenship or participation in a WIA Title I-financially assisted program or activity. Section 188 of WIA is enforced by the Civil Rights Center.

The Pregnancy Discrimination Act of 1978

The Pregnancy Discrimination Act is an amendment to Title VII of the Civil Rights Act of 1964. Discrimination on the basis of pregnancy, childbirth or related medical conditions constitutes unlawful sex discrimination under Title VII. Women affected by pregnancy or related conditions must be treated in the same manner as other applicants or employees with similar abilities or limitations.

 Hiring

An employer cannot refuse to hire a woman because of her pregnancy related condition as long as she is able to perform the major functions of her job. An employer cannot refuse to hire her because of its prejudices against pregnant workers or the prejudices of co-workers, clients or customers.

Pregnancy and Maternity Leave

An employer may not single out pregnancy related conditions for special procedures to determine an employee's ability to work. However, an employer may use any procedure used to screen other employees' ability to work. For example, if an employer requires its employees to submit a doctor's statement concerning their inability to work before granting leave or paying sick benefits, the employer may require employees affected by pregnancy related conditions to submit such statements.

If an employee is temporarily unable to perform her job due to pregnancy, the employer must treat her the same as any other temporarily disabled employee; for example, by providing modified tasks, alternative assignments, disability leave or leave without pay.

Pregnant employees must be permitted to work as long as they are able to perform their jobs. If an employee has been absent from work as a result of a pregnancy related condition and recovers, her employer may not require her to remain on leave until the baby's birth. An employer may not have a rule which prohibits an employee from returning to work for a predetermined length of time after childbirth.

Employers must hold open a job for a pregnancy related absence the same length of time jobs are held open for employees on sick or disability leave.

 Health Insurance

Any health insurance provided by an employer must cover expenses for pregnancy related conditions on the same basis as costs for other medical conditions. Health insurance for expenses arising from abortion is not required, except where the life of the mother is endangered.

Pregnancy related expenses should be reimbursed exactly as those incurred for other medical conditions, whether payment is on a fixed basis or a percentage of reasonable and customary charge basis.

The amounts payable by the insurance provider can be limited only to the same extent as costs for other conditions. No additional, increased or larger deductible can be imposed.

Employers must provide the same level of health benefits for spouses of male employees as they do for spouses of female employees.

 Fringe Benefits

Pregnancy related benefits cannot be limited to married employees. In an all-female workforce or job classification, benefits must be provided for pregnancy related conditions if benefits are provided for other medical conditions.

If an employer provides any benefits to workers on leave, the employer must provide the same benefits for those on leave for pregnancy related conditions.

Employees with pregnancy related disabilities must be treated the same as other temporarily disabled employees for accrual and crediting of seniority, vacation calculation, pay increases and temporary disability benefits.

 Ethnic and Sex Discrimination

Title VII of the Civil Rights Act of 1964 prohibits discrimination in hiring, promotion, discharge, pay, fringe benefits, job training, classification, referral, and other aspects of employment, on the basis of race, color, religion, sex or national origin. This law is enforced by the Equal Employment Opportunity Commission (EEOC).

Title VI of the Civil Rights Act of 1964 prohibits discrimination on the basis of race, color, or national origin in programs and activities that receive federal financial assistance. This law is enforced by the Civil Rights Center.

Title IX of the Education Amendments of 1972 prohibits discrimination on the basis of sex in educational programs and activities that receive federal financial assistance. This law is enforced by the Civil Rights Center.

Sexual Harassment

Sexual harassment is a form of sex discrimination that violates Title VII of the Civil Rights Act of 1964. Title VII applies to employers with 15 or more employees, including state and local governments. It also applies to employment agencies and to labor organizations, as well as to the federal government.

Unwelcome sexual advances, requests for sexual favors, and other verbal or physical conduct of a sexual nature constitute sexual harassment when this conduct explicitly or implicitly affects an individual's employment, unreasonably interferes with an individual's work performance, or creates an intimidating, hostile, or offensive work environment.

Sexual harassment can occur in a variety of circumstances, including but not limited to the following:

- The victim as well as the harasser may be a woman or a man. The victim does not have to be of the opposite sex.

- The harasser can be the victim's supervisor, an agent of the employer, a supervisor in another area, a co-worker, or a non-employee.

- The victim does not have to be the person harassed but could be anyone affected by the offensive conduct.

- Unlawful sexual harassment may occur without economic injury to or discharge of the victim.

- The harasser's conduct must be unwelcome.

It is helpful for the victim to inform the harasser directly that the conduct is unwelcome and must stop. The victim should use any employer complaint mechanism or grievance system available.

When investigating allegations of sexual harassment, EEOC looks at the whole record: the circumstances, such as the nature of the sexual advances, and the context in which the alleged incidents occurred. A determination on the allegations is made from the facts on a case-by-case basis.

Prevention is the best tool to eliminate sexual harassment in the workplace. Employers are encouraged to take steps necessary to prevent sexual harassment from occurring. They should clearly communicate to employees that sexual harassment will not be tolerated. They can do so by providing sexual harassment training to their employees and by establishing an effective complaint or grievance process and taking immediate and appropriate action when an employee complains.

It is also unlawful to retaliate against an individual for opposing employment practices that discriminate based on sex or for filing a discrimination charge, testifying, or participating in any way in an investigation, proceeding, or litigation under Title VII.

 # Affirmative Action

The Department of Labor's Employment Standards Administration's Office of Federal Contract Compliance Programs (OFCCP) enforces the **Executive Order 11246**, as amended; Section 503 of the Rehabilitation Act of 1973, as amended and the affirmative action provisions (Section 4212) of the Vietnam Era Veterans' Readjustment Assistance Act, as amended. Taken together, these laws ban discrimination and require Federal contractors and subcontractors to take affirmative action to ensure that all individuals have an equal opportunity for employment, without regard to race, color, religion, sex, national origin, disability or status as a Vietnam era or special disabled veteran.

OFCP's jurisdiction covers approximately 26 million or nearly 22% of the total civilian workforce (92,500 non-construction establishments and 100,000 construction establishments). The Federal Government awarded more than $179 billion tax-payer dollars in prime contracts in Fiscal Year 1995.

OFCCP requires a contractor, as a condition of having a federal contract, to engage in a self-analysis for the purpose of discovering any barriers to equal employment opportunity. No other Government agency conducts comparable systemic reviews of employers' employment practices to ferret out discrimination. OFCCP also investigates complaints of discrimination.

Each contracting agency in the Executive Branch of government must include the equal opportunity clause in each of its nonexempt government contracts. The equal opportunity clause requires that the contractor will take affirmative action to ensure that applicants are employed, and that employees are treated during employment, without regard to their race, color, religion, sex or national origin. American Indian or Alaskan Native, Asian or Pacific Islander, Black, and Hispanic individuals are considered minorities for purposes of the Executive Order. This clause makes equal employment opportunity and affirmative action integral elements of a contractor's agreement with the government. Failure to comply with the non-discrimination or affirmative action provisions is a violation of the contract.

A contractor in violation of E.O. 11246 may have its contracts canceled, terminated, or suspended in whole or in part, and the contractor may be debarred, i.e., declared ineligible for future government contracts. However, a contractor cannot be debarred without being afforded the opportunity for a full evidentiary hearing. Debarments may be for an indefinite term or for a fixed term. When an indefinite term debarment is imposed, the contractor may be reinstated as soon as it has demonstrated that the violations have been remedied. A fixed-term debarment establishes a trial period during which a contractor can demonstrate its commitment and ability to establish personnel practices that are in compliance with the Executive Order.

If a matter is not resolved through conciliation, OFCCP may refer the matter to the Office of the Solicitor of Labor, which is authorized to institute administrative enforcement proceedings. After a full evidentiary hearing, a Department of Labor Administrative Law Judges issues recommended findings of fact, conclusions of law, and a recommended order. On the basis of the entire record, the Secretary of Labor issues a final Administrative Order. Cases also may be referred to the Department of Justice for judicial enforcement of E.O. 11246, primarily when use of the sanctions authorized by the Order is impracticable, such as a case involving a sole source supplier.

The regulations implementing the Executive Order establish different affirmative action provision for non-construction (i.e., service and supply) contractors and for construction contractors.

Executive Order Affirmative Action Requirements for Supply and Service Contractors Non-construction (service and supply) contractors with 50 or more employees and government contracts of $50,000 or more are required, under Executive Order 11246, to develop and implement a written affirmative action program (AAP) for each establishment. The regulations define an AAP as a set of specific and result-oriented procedures to which a contractor commits itself to apply every good faith effort. The AAP is developed by the contractor (with technical assistance from OFCCP if requested) to assist the contractor in a self-audit of its workforce. The AAP is kept on file and carried out by the contractor; it is submitted to OFCCP only if the agency requests it for the purpose of conducting a compliance review.

The AAP identifies those areas, if any, in the contractor's workforce that reflect utilization of women and minorities. The regulations at 41 CFR 60-2.11 (b) define under-utilization as having fewer minorities or women in a particular job group than would reasonably be expected by their availability. When determining availability of women and minorities, contractors consider, among other factors, the presence of minorities and women having requisite skills in an area in which the contractor can reasonable recruit.

Based on the utilization analyses under Executive Order 11246 and the availability of qualified individuals, the contractors establish goals to reduce or overcome the under-utilization. Good faith efforts may include expanded efforts in outreach, recruitment, training and other activities to increase the pool of qualified minorities and females. The actual selection decision is to be made on a non-discriminatory basis.

For Construction Contractors

OFCCP has established a distinct approach to affirmative action for the construction industry due to the fluid and temporary nature of the construction workforce. In contrast to the service and supply affirmative action program, OFCCP, rather than the contractor, establishes goals and specifies affirmative action which must be undertaken by Federal and federally assisted construction contractors. OFCCP issued specific national goals for women. The female goal of 6.9 percent was extended indefinitely in 1980 and remains in effect today. Construction contractors are not required to develop written affirmative action programs. The regulations enumerate the good faith steps construction contractors must take in order to increase the utilization of minorities and women in the skilled trades.

The numerical goals are established based on the availability of qualified applicants in the job market or qualified candidates in the employer's work force. Executive Order numerical goals do not create set-asides for specific groups, nor are they designed to achieve proportional representation or equal results. Rather, the goal-setting process in affirmative action planning is used to target and measure the effectiveness of affirmative action efforts to eradicate and prevent discrimination. The Executive Order and its supporting regulations do not authorize OFCCP to penalize contractors for not meeting goals. The regulations at 41 CFR 60-2.12(e), 60-2.30 and 60-2.15, specifically prohibit quota and preferential hiring and promotions under the guise of affirmative action numerical goals. In other words, discrimination in the selection decision is prohibited.

OFCCP federal affirmative action in action is exemplified by the EEO programs of the award recipients of the Department of Labor Secretary's Opportunity 2000 Award and Exemplary Voluntary Efforts (EVE) awards. Each year, these awards are given to contractors with outstanding affirmative action programs. Affirmative action refers to the aggressive recruitment programs, mentoring, training, and family programs that work to recruit and retain qualified individuals. Corporate programs nominated for a

Secretary 2000 or EVE award include innovative outreach and recruitment, employee development, management development and employee support programs

OFCCP efforts benefit real people through systemic contractor investigations and through partnerships with private industry and state and local agencies.

In general, OFCCP programs helped many Fortune 1,000 companies and other major corporations break the glass ceiling for women and minorities. In 1970, women accounted for 10.2 percent of the officials and managers reported on the Employer Information Report (EEO-1) form submitted by federal contractors. In 1993, women were 29.9 percent of all officials and managers, according to the EEO-1 data.

Many minorities and women have gained access to employment on large construction projects because of the Department's construction mega-projects. For example, on the Oakland Federal Building project, eight percent of the hours worked on the site were by women. On the New York Federal Courthouse project, 35 percent of the hours were worked by minorities and approximately six percent by women. In addition, OFCCP has recognized the affirmative action efforts of award recipient construction contractors like the Hyman Construction of Manhattan, New York and the Law Company of Kansas.

Working women moved from welfare to forklift operator jobs and other non-traditional construction jobs in Philadelphia and Chicago through OFCCP outreach efforts.

Native Americans are now employed on federal highway construction projects in conjunction with the Council for Tribal Employment Rights and the Cheyenne River Sioux Tribe. Both received Department EPIC awards for their efforts.

More than 70 individuals with disabilities have been employed in computer positions in Columbus, Ohio through a partnership between the department and Goodwill Industries. This cooperative agreement has resulted in prototypes of workplaces specifically designed to welcome persons with severe disabilities.

After highly publicized cases in which veterans were unaware of job openings, a Seattle company hired a specialist to address Vietnam-era veterans' issues.

Because of affirmative action requirements, federal contractors are reviewing their employment policies, including compensation systems, and training their managers and supervisors to identify and correct discrimination and harassment in the workplace.

OFCCP uncovers examples of discrimination every day during its compliance evaluations, including the following incidents:

A hostile working environment at an aircraft maintenance facility, including racial slurs, sexually inappropriate statements, graffiti on bathroom walls, offensive drawings in the workplace, and racial jokes.

Black professionals required to scrub toilets and subjected to racial harassment.

An individual with a disability (Native American amputee) was subjected to verbal harassment because of his disability, physically assaulted, and denied benefits and opportunities provided his non-disabled colleagues.

Affirmative action is necessary to prevent discrimination and to address stereotypical thinking and biases that still impede employment opportunity.

Overall findings from a DOL survey found that women advanced more quickly in contractor firms than in non-contractor firms.

Federal contractors have changed the corporate climate in ways that are not statistically measurable because of the requirements of Executive Order 11246 and other laws enforced by OFCCP. For example, corporations now post job announcements and do not rely solely on word of mouth recruitment. Corporate sensitivity to issues like sex and race harassment and wage discrimination has increased, as has the awareness of the benefits of a family friendly environment. Employers now view ability, not disability.

As you have read above, there are two main strategies to affirmative action. A quota-based strategy, which is when you set a specific number of new hires as a goal for hiring strategies and the promotion of minorities and women. The second is a good faith effort strategy. This is when the employer evaluates their current way of doing business and adjusts their policies and culture to be accepting to those groups and to ensure that nothing impedes their path to success.

The 4/5 Rule

The 4/5 rule is a tool that has been developed to help prevent discrimination. This is a tool that larger employers, staffing firms and other groups use to determine whether there is discrimination in the selection (hiring process).

To figure out the 4/5 (or 80%) rule you need to complete some simple arithmetic.

1. Calculate the rate of selection for each applicant group (divide the number of persons selected from a group by the number of applicants from that group).

2. Observe which group has the highest selection rate.

3. Calculate the impact ratios, by comparing the selection rate for each group with that of the highest group (divide the selection rate for a group by the selection rate for the highest group).

4. Observe whether the selection rate for any group is substantially less (i.e., usually less than 4/5ths or 80%) than the selection rate for the highest group. If it is, adverse impact is indicated in most circumstances.

Applicants	Hired	Selection Rate Percent Hired
80 Black	48	48/80 or 60%
40 Asian	12	12/40 or 30%

Civil Rights Act of 1991

The Civil Rights Act of 1991 was created to ease the burden on employees who were suing for discrimination. The employer now has to prove that a job qualification is in fact a business necessity or a necessary qualification. The act also gives the employee access to a jury trial and the right for damages (monetary) against the employer.

 HIPPA

The Health Insurance Portability and Accountability Act (HIPAA) provides rights and protections for participants and beneficiaries in group health plans. HIPAA includes protections for coverage under group health plans that limit exclusions for preexisting conditions; prohibits discrimination against employees and dependents based on their health status; and allows a special opportunity to enroll in a new plan to individuals in certain circumstances. HIPAA may also give you a right to purchase individual coverage if you have no group health plan coverage available, and have exhausted COBRA or other continuation coverage.

 WARN

The Worker Adjustment and Retraining Notification Act (WARN) protects workers, their families, and communities by requiring most employers with 100 or more employees to provide notification 60 calendar days in advance of plant closings and mass layoffs.

Employees entitled to notice under WARN include managers and supervisors, as well as hourly and salaried workers. WARN requires that notice also be given to employees' representatives, the local chief elected official, and the state dislocated worker unit.

Advance notice gives workers and their families some transition time to adjust to the prospective loss of employment, to seek and obtain other jobs, and, if necessary, to enter skill training or retraining that will allow these workers to compete successfully in the job market.

Generally, WARN covers employers with 100 or more employees, not counting those who have worked less than six months in the last 12 months and those who work an average of less than 20 hours a week.

Regular federal, state, and local government entities that provide public services are not covered by WARN. The Department of Labor's (DOL) Employment and Training Administration (ETA) administers WARN at the federal level, and some states have plant closure laws of their own.

DOL has no enforcement role in seeking damages for workers who did not receive adequate notice of a layoff or received no notice at all. However, they can assist workers in finding a new job or learning about training opportunities that may be available.

Unemployment Insurance

Unemployment insurance is a state-by-state mandated program which requires employers to contribute to an unemployment insurance fund. This provides weekly pay to employees who lose their job through layoffs, closures, etc. Those who are "justifiably" terminated are not eligible for the benefit.

Safety and Health

AIDS in the workplace is a small concern for most industries. Information on employees who have contracted AIDS is generally not disclosed unless the nature of the job could result in injury, where the coworkers who may treat the peer would require knowledge of their condition in order to protect themselves. This is most commonly corrected by the use of rubber gloves in all situations where blood is present.

Stress in the Workplace

Stress is our response to any change. A stressor is anything that causes us to have to adjust to a new situation or change. Adjustment is the term for what we use to cope. For example, someone who handles stress poorly could drink alcohol excessively to compensate or to escape. Strain is what happens to our bodies when we get stressed. Eustress is stress that we can use positively for our personal growth. Some examples of eustress are: getting married, starting a new school or job. Distress is stress that can have a negative effect on us. Some examples of distress are injury, problems with others, financial problems, or the death of a loved one.

We can also be stressed by our environment. Examples of environmental stress are background stressors like air pollution or noise pollution, like when a co-worker is playing his or her radio. You may be unaware of environmental stressors, but they are still present and may cause strain.

Managing stress can seem overwhelming but there are many things we can do to control it or to harness it to good use. When you realize thoughts that are irrational, like worrying about things that are not likely going to happen, you can identify those thoughts and rationally discount them.

Exercise and relaxation are critical positive ways to deal with stress. Eating right will also help you deal with stress – either through the placebo effect of comfort food or by having a healthy diet, which will allow your body to be in top shape.

Managing time is also an effective way to deal with stress. Prioritize your tasks, clean off your desk, do those little things you've been putting off. These cause strain in the back of your mind, creating stress you aren't even aware of having. Some alternative techniques to relieve stress include hypnosis, massage, meditation and biofeedback. The lesser known of these areas, bio feedback is simply a process of self-monitoring through a machine the heart rate, blood pressure, etc., and learning to mentally control these factors.

Railway Labor Act

The railway labor act was one of the first of it's kind in dealing with workers and their employers. This was the first federal law to address labor issues for laborers that worked on the railways. The RLA guaranteed the right for workers to join or not join unions at their choice, without threat of coercion from their employers. The creation of the RLA was intended to minimize the impact of strikes on the main major source of transportation at the time, rail or train. This act still exists today and is used to govern labor relations in rail and air transportation.

Collective Bargaining and Unions

Unions are formal associations of employees formed with a view to represent those employees in any dialogue to bargain collectively with the management. Their negotiations with the management include improved working conditions, better wage structures, less hours of work, more rest periods, etc., and generally work towards establishing good labor policies. In the USA 'organized' labor is a term normally used to distinguish members of unions from employees who do not have a formal union to support them. There are blue-collar as well as white-collar worker unions in the USA.

Unions use a process of discussion or negotiation between management and the union that represents the workers. Each side comes to the table with their own agenda and through time and compromise, reaches an agreement. This is a simplified version as most contracts take several rounds of negotiations regarding wages, etc. Once a formal agreement is reached both parties sign a typed contract. In these sessions, an arbitrator may be used. The arbitrator takes on the role of a judge and can determine what is "fair." An arbitrator also generally has the last word and has the power to complete the settlement. A mediator is a neutral third party that helps two parties reach an agreement. They do not have any power to "force" the sides to agree but help to keep negotiations on track. If the union decides to not negotiate anymore they call a "strike" where the workers do not come to work until the problem is resolved.

In reality, unions are mostly a thing of the past. Although they exist in some "trade" capacities still today, they actually hinder the American worker by not giving them the power to negotiate for themselves. If you manage union employees and you need to talk to them about their performance, you do not speak to them. Instead, you speak to the union and they speak to them for you. It adds an additional layer to the communication process, making it harder for businesses to manage their employees.

Also, unions involve dues which the member must pay. Unions also contribute to political groups and candidates whose views may or may not be the views of the member. The member does not have control over where his dues go or to whom they go.

Union groups are called "shops" instead of being called a company. A union shop can hire nonunion workers but they must pay dues and join the union within a set period of time. Some union shops are "closed shops"; they only hire union members. Although this is against the law, it still happens today. An agency shop includes member and nonmembers of the union but all are require to pay dues. Open shop is when they have both members and nonmembers work together, but only the union members pay dues.

The AFL-CIO or American Federation of Labor and Congress of Industrial Organizations is the large political body for unions. By voluntarily belonging to this organization, the members are receiving the benefits of their lobbying power in politics.

Union Member Rights

Bill of Rights - Union members have:
- Equal rights to participate in union activities
- Freedom of speech and assembly
- A voice in setting rates of dues, fees, and assessments
- Protection of the right to sue
- Safeguards against improper discipline

Copies of Collective Bargaining Agreements - Union members and nonunion employees have the right to receive or inspect copies of collective bargaining agreements.

Reports - Unions are required to file an initial information report, copies of constitutions and bylaws, and an annual financial report with OLMS. Unions must make the reports available to members and permit members to examine supporting records for just cause.

Officer Elections - Union members have the right to:
- Nominate candidates for office
- Run for office
- Cast a secret ballot
- Protest the conduct of an election

Officer Removal - Local union members have the right to an adequate procedure for the removal of an elected officer guilty of serious misconduct.

Trusteeships - Unions may only be placed in trusteeship by a parent body for the reasons specified in the LMRDA.

Prohibition Against Certain Discipline - A union or any of its officials may not fine, expel, or otherwise discipline a member for exercising any LMRDA right.

Prohibition Against Violence - No one may use or threaten to use force or violence to interfere with a union member in the exercise of LMRDA rights.

Union Officer Responsibilities

Financial Safeguards - Union officers have a duty to manage the funds and property of the union solely for the benefit of the union and its members in accordance with the union's constitution and bylaws. Union officers or employees who embezzle or steal union funds or other assets commit a Federal crime punishable by a fine and/or imprisonment.

Bonding - Union officers or employees who handle union funds or property must be bonded to provide protection against losses if their union has property and annual financial receipts which exceed $5,000.

Officer Reports - Union officers and employees must file reports concerning any loans and benefits received from, or certain financial interests in, employers whose employees their unions represent and businesses that deal with their unions.

Officer Elections - Unions must:

- Hold elections of officers of local unions by secret ballot at least every three years
- Conduct regular elections in accordance with their constitution and bylaws and preserve all records for one year
- Mail a notice of election to every member at least 15 days prior to the election
- Comply with a candidate's request to distribute campaign material
- Not use union funds or resources to promote any candidate (nor may employer funds or resources be used)
- Permit candidates to have election observers
- Allow candidates to inspect the union's membership list once within 30 days prior to the election

Restrictions on Holding Office - A person convicted of certain crimes may not serve as a union officer, employee, or other representative of a union for up to 13 years.

Loans - A union may not have outstanding loans to any one officer or employee that in total exceed $2,000 at any time.

Fines - A union may not pay the fine of any officer or employee convicted of any willful violation of the LMRDA.

NLRA and NLRB

The National Labor Relations Board is an independent federal agency created by Congress in 1935 to administer the National Labor Relations Act (NLRA), the primary law governing relations between unions and employers in the private sector. The statute guarantees the right of employees to organize and to bargain collectively with their employers or to refrain from all such activity. Generally applying to all employers involved in interstate commerce--other than airlines, railroads, agriculture, and government--the Act implements the national labor policy of assuring free choice and encouraging collective bargaining as a means of maintaining industrial peace. Through the years, Congress has amended the Act and the Board and courts have developed a body of law drawn from the statute.

What Does the NLRB Do?
In its statutory assignment, the NLRB has two principal functions: (1) to determine, through [secret-ballot elections,] the free democratic choice by employees whether they wish to be represented by a union in dealing with their employers and if so, by which union; and (2) to prevent and remedy unlawful acts, called [unfair labor practices,] by either employers or unions. The agency does not act on its own motion in either function. It processes only those charges of unfair labor practices and petitions for employee elections that are filed with the NLRB in one of its 51 Regional, Subregional, or Resident Offices.

What Is the NLRB's Structure?
The agency has two major, separate components.

The Board itself has five Members and primarily acts as a quasi-judicial body in deciding cases on the basis of formal records in administrative proceedings. Board Members are appointed by the President to 5-year terms, with Senate consent, the term of one Member expiring each year. The current Members are Robert J. Battista (Chairman), Wilma B. Liebman, Peter C. Schaumber, Peter N. Kirsanow, and Dennis P. Walsh.

The General Counsel, appointed by the President to a 4-year term with Senate consent, is independent from the Board and is responsible for the investigation and prosecution of unfair labor practice cases and for the general supervision of the NLRB field offices in the processing of cases. The current General Counsel is Ronald Meisburg. Each Regional Office is headed by a Regional Director who is responsible for making the initial determination in cases arising within the geographical area served by the region.

How Are Unfair Labor Practice Cases Processed?
When an unfair labor practice (ULP) charge is filed, the appropriate field office conducts an investigation to determine whether there is reasonable cause to believe the Act

has been violated. If the Regional Director determines that the charge lacks merit, it will be dismissed unless the charging party decides to withdraw the charge. A dismissal may be appealed to the General Counsel's office in Washington, D.C.

If the Regional Director finds reasonable cause to believe a violation of the law has been committed, the region seeks a voluntary settlement to remedy the alleged violations. If these settlement efforts fail, a formal complaint is issued and the case goes to hearing before an NLRB Administrative Law Judge. The judge issues a written decision that may be appealed to the five- Member Board in Washington for a final agency determination. The Board's decision is subject to review in a U.S. Court of Appeals. Depending upon the nature of the case, the General Counsel's goal is to complete investigations and, where further proceedings are warranted, issue complaints if settlement is not reached within 7 to 15 weeks from the filing of the charge. Of the total ULP charges filed each year [about 25,000], approximately one-third are found to have merit of which over 90% are settled.

Sample Test Questions

1) John Turner was laid off from his communications job. What law gave him the right to continue receiving health benefits by paying the monthly premium?

    A) OSHA
    B) ADA
    C) COBRA
    D) ERISA

The correct answer is C:) COBRA. The Comprehensive Omnibus Budget Reconciliation Act allows employees to retain medical insurance after they quit or are terminated, for up to 18 months.

2) The most valuable asset a company has is managed by the

    A) CEO
    B) CFO
    C) HR Manager
    D) Marketing Manager

The correct answer is C:) HR Manager. An organization's most valuable asset is its employees which are managed by the HR Manager.

3) When a new employee is hired it is part of which process?

    A) Training
    B) Selection
    C) Termination
    D) Development

The correct answer is B:) Selection. Selection means hiring, as in "selecting" a new employee.

4) HR Managers make policies _____ with the mission statement.

    A) Disagree
    B) Vary
    C) Congruent
    D) Conflict

The correct answer is C:) Congruent. HR Managers have a responsibility to make policies congruent (in line with) the company's mission statement.

5) Which of the following is a specific, scientific way of categorizing exactly what a skills and tasks a specific job requires?

    A) Job analysis
    B) Job creation
    C) Job design
    D) Job relatedness

The correct answer is A:) Job analysis. Job analysis is a way to justify a job description by categorizing exactly what a skills and tasks a specific job requires.

6) John is writing out the ideal traits for the new computer engineer he wants to hire. What process is he using?

    A) Job analysis
    B) Job creation
    C) Job design
    D) Job relatedness

The correct answer is C:) Job design. Job design a listing of the ideal traits for a position.

7) If you are an authoritarian, you ascribe to

    A) Theory X
    B) Theory Y
    C) Theory XY
    D) Management theory

The correct answer is A:) Theory X.

8) Which of the following would not show job relatedness for a plumber?

    A) Plumbing license
    B) City of residence
    C) Ownership of tools
    D) Driving record

The correct answer is B:) City of residence. The city of residence cannot be a factor in job relatedness for a plumber. If he is able to commute to the job site, he is able to perform the job. Licenses, tools and driving record are all requirements that are legally justifiable.

9) Which of the following is NOT a part of the recruiting process?

    A) Posting jobs online
    B) Interviewing
    C) Employee referrals
    D) Radio advertisement advertising openings

The correct answer is B:) Interviewing. Interviewing is part of the selection, not the recruiting process.

10) Using a headhunter to find eligible candidates means

    A) You will be guaranteed an employee
    B) You will pay 30-40% of the future salary as a premium
    C) You will find all male employees
    D) You will have less prospects than not using a headhunter

The correct answer is B:) You will pay 30-40% of the future salary as a premium. If you hire through a headhunter, generally you are paying a premium which could be 30 to 40% of the new hire's salary.

11) Which of the following shows how essential job tasks are related to the job?

    A) Job analysis
    B) Job creation
    C) Job design
    D) Job relatedness

The correct answer is D:) Job relatedness. Job relatedness shows how essential job tasks are related to the job.

12) Which of the following is NOT a word that signifies someone leaving the organization?

    A) Termination
    B) Turnover
    C) Pink slip
    D) Turningpoint

The correct answer is D:) Turningpoint. Termination, turnover and pink slips are all ways to describe a reduction in force.

13) What is the best predictor of future performance?

    A) Education
    B) Punctuality
    C) Past performance
    D) Management training

The correct answer is C:) Past performance. The best predictor of future performance is by analyzing past performance.

14) When a test is devised to correlate an employee's work habits with performance it is called?

    A) Criterion-related validity test
    B) Predictive validity test
    C) Concurrent validity test
    D) Cross-validation test

The correct answer is A:) Criterion-related validity test. A criterion-related validity test is created to test an employee's work habits and match that with performance.

15) When you verify the results from a study by using a sample group it is called

    A) Criterion-related validity test
    B) Predictive validity test
    C) Concurrent validity test
    D) Cross-validation test

The correct answer is D:) Cross-validation test. A cross-validation test ensures that the conclusions drawn from research are correct.

16) When a group of current employees are rated on a set of skills by their manager and then given a skills test, this is called a

    A) Criterion-related validity test
    B) Predictive validity test
    C) Concurrent validity test
    D) Cross-validation test

The correct answer is C:) Concurrent validity test. A concurrent validity test is when current employees are rated on a set of skills by their manager and then given a skills test while management monitors the gap between the perceived performance and the true performance on the test.

17) Which of the following tests is analyzed after the employee is hired

    A) Criterion-related validity test
    B) Predictive validity test
    C) Concurrent validity test
    D) Cross-validation test

The correct answer is B:) Predictive validity test. In a predictive validity test, an applicant is tested, hired, then evaluated by their current supervisor. Later their original test scores are compared with the supervisor's evaluations.

18) The value in the Delphi technique lies in the _____ it creates.

    A) Information
    B) Conversation
    C) Thinking
    D) Ideas

The correct answer is D:) Ideas. Though the goal is to obtain a single expert opinion, the new ideas and differing opinions that often form are also valuable.

19) Which of the following is the theory of autonomy that depends on a corporation's approach to globalization?

    A) Limited autonomy
    B) Variable autonomy
    C) Negotiable autonomy
    D) Dependant autonomy

The correct answer is A:) Limited autonomy. There are three theories concerning subsidiary's autonomy in decision-making.

20) What is the main goal of a quality circle?

    A) To meet the goals of manufacturing processes efficiently
    B) To review the quality of products and identify product design flaws
    C) To solve problems and generate improvement in the workplace
    D) All of the above

The correct answer is C:) To solve problems and generate improvement in the workplace. Quality circles are designed to identify problems and to create solutions.

21) Which test concludes the capacity a person has to learn new skills?

    A) Aptitude test
    B) Attitude test
    C) Achievement test
    D) Analogous test

The correct answer is A:) Aptitude test. An aptitude test determines the capacity a person has to learn new information or new skills.

22) Past performance is the best predictor of future behavior. Which of the following applies that in an interview format?

    A) Job interview
    B) Performance interview
    C) Behavioral description interview
    D) None of the above

The correct answer is C:) Behavioral description interview. A behavioral description interview gives candidates a chance to show how they dealt with certain situations in the past. Because past performance is the best predictor of future performance, it shows the interviewer how they will perform if hired.

23) Which of the following investigates businesses and individuals for enforcement of laws regarding protected classes?

    A) OSHA
    B) EEO
    C) Department of Labor
    D) COBRA

The correct answer is B:) EEO.

24) When given a hypothetical situation in an interview it is called?

    A) Situational interview
    B) Behavioral description interview
    C) Structured interview
    D) Performance interview

The correct answer is A:) Situational interview. Situational interviews are when candidates are given hypothetical situations and asked how they would respond.

25) When an employee is given assistance finding a new job it is called

    A) Pink slip
    B) Reduction in force
    C) Downsizing
    D) Outplacement

The correct answer is D:) Outplacement. When an employee is given assistance finding a new job it is called outplacement.

26) When someone permanently will lose their job through a reduction of the company it is called

    A) Job sharing
    B) Telecommuting
    C) Downsizing
    D) Outplacement

The correct answer is C:) Downsizing. When someone permanently will lose their job through a reduction of the company it is called downsizing. Reduction in force means the same thing.

27) When there is not enough work to be done and employees are temporarily or permanently left without work it is called

    A) Reduction in force
    B) Outplacement
    C) Downsizing
    D) Layoff

The correct answer is D:) Layoff. When there is not enough work to be done and employees are left without work it is called a layoff. This can be a temporary or permanent situation.

28) What is it called when you learn the job by actually doing it?

    A) On-the-job training
    B) Vestibule training
    C) Job instruction training
    D) Programmed learning

The correct answer is A:) On-the-job training. On the job training is when you learn the job by actually doing it.

29) Which of the following is NOT a factor with job satisfaction?

    A) Hours
    B) Pay
    C) Benefits
    D) Vacation location

The correct answer is D:) Vacation location.

30) What is it called when the employee is taught information, asked questions, and reviews the answers with the trainer?

    A) On-the-job training
    B) Vestibule training
    C) Job instruction training
    D) Programmed learning

The correct answer is D:) Programmed learning. Programmed learning is when the employee is taught information, asked questions, and reviews the answers with the trainer.

31) Which of the following is a step-by-step method of teaching a job?

    A) On-the-job training
    B) Vestibule training
    C) Job instruction training
    D) Programmed learning

The correct answer is C:) Job instruction training. Job instruction training is a step-by-step method of teaching a job.

32) John trains in "fake" restaurant to prepare for his new job at a "real restaurant," this is called what type of training?

    A) On-the-job training
    B) Vestibule training
    C) Job instruction training
    D) Programmed learning

The correct answer is B:) Vestibule training. Vestibule training is when employees are trained in an offsite facility that mimics the job environment.

33) Which of the following is NOT considered on-the-job training?

    A) Planned progression
    B) Temporary promotion
    C) Job rotation
    D) Conference

The correct answer is D:) Conference. Attending a conference is considered off-the-job training.

34) Which of the following is NOT off-the-job training?

    A) Programmed learning
    B) Conference
    C) Job rotation
    D) Role-playing

The correct answer is C:) Job rotation. Job rotation is when you learn a new job by rotating with other employees. Because you are learning while on the job this is considered on-the-job training.

35) Which of the following rates employees on a list of traits or job requirements?

    A) Alternation ranking method
    B) Paired comparison method
    C) Behaviorally anchored rating scale
    D) Graphic rating scale method

The correct answer is D:) Graphic rating scale method. The graphic rating scale method rates employees on a list of traits or job requirements.

36) What is it called when you compare each employee to every other employee in a particular area?

    A) Alternation ranking method
    B) Paired comparison method
    C) Behaviorally anchored rating scale
    D) Graphic rating scale method

The correct answer is B:) Paired comparison method. Paired comparison method compares each employee to every other employee in a particular area.

37) Which of the following rates employees as a group from best to worst on a particular area?

    A) Alternation ranking method
    B) Paired comparison method
    C) Behaviorally anchored rating scale
    D) Graphic rating scale method

The correct answer is A:) Alternation ranking method. Alternation ranking method rates employees as a group from best to worst on a particular area.

38) Which of the following is the Title that protects race?

    A) Title IV
    B) Title V
    C) Title VI
    D) Title VII

The correct answer is D:) Title VII.

39) Dual career ladder programs are designed for employees who

   A) Have technical skills and also want to work in a managerial capacity
   B) Have managerial skills and also want to work in a technical capacity
   C) Have technical skills and do not want to work in a managerial capacity
   D) Have managerial skills and do not want to work in a technical capacity

The correct answer is C:) Have technical skills and do not want to work in a managerial capacity.

40) The Equal Pay Act of 1963 prevents pay discrimination related to

   A) Salary only
   B) Salary and job-related expenses
   C) Salary, job-related expenses, and benefits
   D) Salary, job-related expenses, benefits, and bonuses

The correct answer is D:) Salary, job-related expenses, benefits and bonuses. "Pay" includes salary, overtime, insurance, vacation and holiday pay, cleaning or gas allowances, hotel accommodations, reimbursement for travel expenses, benefits, stock options, bonus plans, profit sharing, and bonuses.

41) What is it called when ratings are matched with employee behavior?

   A) Alternation ranking method
   B) Paired comparison method
   C) Behaviorally anchored rating scale
   D) Graphic rating scale method

The correct answer is C:) Behaviorally anchored rating scale. The behaviorally anchored rating scale matches rating with employee behavior.

42) When employees are judged by specific goals and if they met their goals this is called

   A) Classification method
   B) Forced distribution method
   C) Management by objectives
   D) Critical incident method

The correct answer is C:) Management by objectives. When employees are managed, rewarded and penalized by meeting goals it is called management by objectives.

43) Grades are defined by the requirements found to be common to several tasks spanning different departments resulting in what system?

A) Classification method
B) Forced distribution method
C) Management by objectives
D) Critical incident method

The correct answer is A:) Classification method. The classification method defines and assigns grades.

44) Grouping employees in specific groups and grading their efforts on the curve is called what?

A) Classification method
B) Forced distribution method
C) Management by objectives
D) Critical incident method

The correct answer is B:) Forced distribution method. Forced distribution method is when employees are put in specific groups then their efforts are graded on the curve.

45) Which of the following is the second step when forming a group?

A) Storming
B) Norming
C) Forming
D) Conforming

The correct answer is A:) Storming.

46) John comes to work late many times a month. His supervisor keeps track of these tardies as well as when he exceeds his goals. What method is being used?

A) Classification method
B) Forced distribution method
C) Management by objectives
D) Critical incident method

The correct answer is D:) Critical incident method. The critical incident method is when management keeps a record of an employee's positive or negative behavior.

47) Which of the following ensures that employees retain access to medical coverage after involuntary termination?

    A) OSHA
    B) EEO
    C) Department of Labor
    D) COBRA

The correct answer is D:) COBRA.

48) Which of the following is NOT part of TQM, Total Quality Management?

    A) Doing things right the first time
    B) Taking ownership of issues
    C) Continually improving
    D) Understanding the customer's needs

The correct answer is B:) Taking ownership of issues. While important, taking ownership of issues is not a key factor of TQM. TQM can be summarized as doing things correctly the first time, continually improving and understanding the customer's needs.

49) A manager who believes that all people are valuable and want to contribute to their best ability you ascribe to

    A) Theory X
    B) Theory Y
    C) Theory XY
    D) Management theory

The correct answer is B:) Theory Y.

50) The United States and what two countries participate in NAFTA?

    A) Mexico and Guatemala
    B) Columbia and Ireland
    C) Canada and Mexico
    D) France and Spain

The correct answer is C:) Canada and Mexico. Canada, Mexico and the United States are the three countries that are involved with NAFTA, the North American Free Trade Agreement.

51) NAFTA allows what between the countries involved?

    A) Free immigration
    B) Trade free from embargoes
    C) No passports required to travel between them
    D) Extra taxation on goods

The correct answer is B:) Trade free from embargoes. NAFTA allows for free trade between Canada, Mexico and the United States.

52) The hay plan is best known as a

    A) Job enrichment plan
    B) Job performance plan
    C) Job sharing plan
    D) Job evaluation plan

The correct answer is D:) Job evaluation plan.

53) What similar system in Europe allows for lessened trade barriers?

    A) EU
    B) APEC
    C) Peace Corps
    D) UN

The correct answer is A:) EU. The European Union helps lessen trade barriers for the countries involved in the Union. APEC is a similar organization in Asia called the Asia Pacific Economic Cooperation.

54) Which of the following is NOT a protected Title VII class?

    A) Race
    B) Age
    C) Sexual preference
    D) Religion

The correct answer is C:) Sexual preference.

55) Social security benefit increases are based on increases in the

    A) Average wage index
    B) Cost of living
    C) Consumer price index
    D) None of the above

The correct answer is B:) Cost of living. Cost of living is measured by the consumer price index.

56) If Jennifer is at a grade 22 and Peter is at a grade 45

    A) They are paid the same
    B) Jennifer is paid more
    C) Peter is paid more
    D) Neither is paid, they are independent contractors

The correct answer is C:) Peter is paid more. Typically, the higher the grade of the position, the higher the pay.

57) If you are getting paid overtime

    A) You receive your regular wages
    B) You receive double wages
    C) You receive time and one half your wages
    D) You are accruing extra vacation time

The correct answer is C:) You receive time and one half your wages. Overtime is paid at one and a half your regular hourly rate.

58) Kyle is a salaried employee. This means

    A) He is not entitled to overtime
    B) He is not entitled to vacation pay
    C) He is not entitled to school/tuition reimbursement
    D) He cannot be fired

The correct answer is A:) He is not entitled to overtime. Generally, salaried employees are not paid overtime. This is because they are paid the same amount every pay period, regardless of the hours worked.

59) Brenda is paid piecework. If she is paid 75 cents for every hat she sows and she sows 15 in one hour, how much is she paid per hour?

   A) $7.50
   B) $8.50
   C) $9.75
   D) $11.25

The correct answer is D:) $11.25. Brenda is paid per piece. $.75 multiplied by 15 is $11.25 an hour.

60) John is paid $1500 per computer he sells. This is his only compensation. This means he

   A) Is paid salary
   B) Is paid on commission
   C) Is paid piecework
   D) Is paid both salary and commission

The correct answer is B:) Is paid on commission. When a person is only paid a percentage or fixed amount based on the amount they sell, it is called commission only.

61) When an employee receives an hourly wage and an extra bonus for each task completed it is called

   A) Salary
   B) Standard hour plan
   C) Commission
   D) None of the above

The correct answer is B:) Standard hour plan. When an employee receives an hourly wage and an extra bonus for each task completed they are on a standard hour plan.

62) Which of the following is responsible for ensuring employee safety?

   A) OSHA
   B) EEO
   C) Department of Labor
   D) COBRA

The correct answer is A:) OSHA.

63) What law/organization protects you from being fired because your wages are being garnished?

    A) ACLU
    B) EEO
    C) CCPA
    D) FLSA

The correct answer is C:) CCPA. Title Three of the CCPA or Consumer Credit Protection Act (CCPA) prohibits an employer from discharging an employee whose earnings have been subject to garnishment for any one debt, regardless of the number of levies made or proceedings brought to collect it.

64) Which of the following in not a benefit

    A) Paid vacation
    B) Paid sick days
    C) Safe work environment
    D) 401k

The correct answer is C:) Safe work environment. A safe work environment is a requirement, not a benefit.

65) Which of the following organizations provides health care on a prepaid basis?

    A) Health Insurance
    B) HMO
    C) 401k
    D) FSA

The correct answer is B:) HMO. While a FSA or Flexible Spending Account is a way to personally prepay your medical expenses, it is not an organization. HMO stands for Health Maintenance Organization.

66) What is it called when an employee receives certain accrued benefits based on years of service?

    A) Termination
    B) Vesting
    C) Early retirement
    D) Silver handshake

The correct answer is B:) Vesting. Vesting is when an employee receives certain accrued benefits based on years of service such as money matched to their 401k account or retirement benefits. Something that has been vested cannot be taken away if an employee quits or is terminated.

67) Joline is having a stressful time at work and problems at home. She can visit a psychologist or other counselor through her employer's _____ program.

    A) EAP
    B) SEOP
    C) FSA
    D) ESOP

The correct answer is A:) EAP. An employee assistance program or EAP gives referrals and/or free counseling to employees in need.

68) Which of the following are barriers to making decisions?

    A) Statistics
    B) Lack of statistics
    C) Emotions
    D) All of the above

The correct answer is D:) All of the above.

69) A 401k account provides what?

    A) A way to save for retirement
    B) A pension account
    C) Stock in the company
    D) None of the above

The correct answer is A:) A way to save for retirement. A 401k is a way to save for retirement. What the employee chooses to contribute is taken out before it is taxed. Many employers match up to 3%, making an employees contribution 6%, helping offset the money needed to retire.

70) Kyle falls of the roof while doing his roofing job. What program will allow him to keep getting his wages while out of work?

    A) Lawsuit
    B) OSHA
    C) Health insurance
    D) Workers' compensation insurance

The correct answer is D:) Workers' compensation insurance. Workers' compensation insurance is required on the state or federal level for all business. This insurance pays worker's hospital bills and lost wages.

71) The Delphi process takes place in what length of time?

    A) The Delphi method is usually a long process that continues as long as necessary to form a consensus.
    B) The Delphi method is usually a long process that continues until the participants reach the correct answer.
    C) The Delphi method is usually a short process that takes no longer than a week.
    D) The Delphi method is usually a short process that takes place in a single day.

The correct answer is A:) The Delphi method is usually a long process that continues as long as necessary to form a consensus.

72) Members of a quality circle

I. Are volunteers
II. Meet on company time
III. Are paid according to their contributions

    A) I and II
    B) II and III
    C) I and III
    D) I, II, and III

The correct answer is A:) I and II.

73) This is a commission that investigates and prosecutes those business and individuals who discriminate against protected classes

    A) EEO
    B) OSHA
    C) FMLA
    D) ERISA

The correct answer is A:) EEO. EEO, Equal Employment Opportunity is a commission that investigates and prosecutes those business and individuals who discriminate against protected classes.

74) _____is a federal law that sets minimum standards for most voluntarily established pension and health plans in private industry to provide protection for individuals in these plans.

    A) EEO
    B) OSHA
    C) FMLA
    D) ERISA

The correct answer is D:) ERISA. The Employee Retirement Income Security Act of 1974 (ERISA) is a federal law that sets minimum standards for most voluntarily established pension and health plans in private industry to provide protection for individuals in these plans.

75) _____ assures the safety and health of America's workers.

    A) EEO
    B) OSHA
    C) FMLA
    D) ERISA

The correct answer is B:) OSHA. OSHA, Occupational Safety & Health Administration, assures the safety and health of America's workers by setting and enforcing standards; providing training, outreach, and education; establishing partnerships; and encouraging continual improvement in workplace safety and health.

76) John is making $23 per hour working at a fast food chain as a cook. He has worked there for six years and received cost of living raises every year. This could be an example of

    A) Salary
    B) EEO
    C) Red circle wages
    D) Job enrichment

The correct answer is C:) Red circle wages. This is when a worker is receiving a wage higher than the maximum salary for a position based on your employee compensation policy or current industry rates.

77) The Big Five personality types are assessed through a test. People with similar scores

    A) Tend to work well together
    B) Should not work together
    C) Do not balance each other out
    D) Two of the above

The correct answer is A:) Tend to work well together. People with similar scores usually have similar work attitudes, similar problem solving methods, and respond well to each other's demeanor.

78) What challenges do unions pose for human resource management?

    A) Accountability assumed for deducting union labor fees
    B) Collective bargaining makes it more complex to handle employee grievances
    C) The necessity to hire an expert in labor law and a union work environment
    D) All of the above

The correct answer is D:) All of the above. Human resource management and unions work best together when both parties are prepared to work together.

79) Which organization/law prohibits discriminating against qualified individuals with disabilities?

A) ADA
B) COBRA
C) Equal Pay Act of 1963
D) Age Discrimination Act of 1975

The correct answer is A:) ADA. The ADA, Americans with Disabilities Act prohibits employers of 15 or more workers, employment agencies, and labor organizations of 15 or more workers from discriminating against qualified individuals with disabilities.

80) Which of the following provides rights and protections for participants and beneficiaries in group health plans?

A) HIPPA
B) WARN
C) Taft Hartley Act
D) ADA

The correct answer is A:) HIPPA. The Health Insurance Portability and Accountability Act (HIPAA) provides rights and protections for participants and beneficiaries in group health plans.

81) Which law/organization requires most employers with 100 or more employees to provide notification 60 calendar days in advance of plant closings and mass layoffs?

A) HIPPA
B) WARN
C) Taft Hartley Act
D) ADA

The correct answer is B:) WARN. The Worker Adjustment and Retraining Notification Act (WARN) protects workers, their families, and communities by requiring most employers with 100 or more employees to provide notification 60 calendar days in advance of plant closings and mass layoffs.

82) Which of the following restricts unions?

    A) HIPPA
    B) WARN
    C) Taft Hartley Act
    D) ADA

The correct answer is C:) Taft Hartley Act. In 1947, Congress passed the Taft Hartley Act which outlawed for unions the closed shop, jurisdictional strikes, secondary boycotts and made additional requirements for unions.

83) Which of the following only applies to companies/unions with 15 or more workers?

    A) HIPPA
    B) WARN
    C) Taft Hartley Act
    D) ADA

The correct answer is D:) ADA. Title I of the Americans with Disabilities Act (ADA) prohibits employers of 15 or more workers, employment agencies, and labor organizations of 15 or more workers from discriminating against qualified individuals with disabilities.

84) Dual career ladder programs are most common in what industry?

    A) Engineering
    B) Scientific
    C) Medical
    D) All of the above

The correct answer is D:) All of the above. All of the above careers offer jobs that provide higher pay for more expertise in the field.

85) The Equal Pay Act protects against pay discrimination based on _____ for employees who perform the same work.

    A) Age
    B) Gender
    C) Race
    D) All of the above

The correct answer is B:) Gender.

86) The Equal Pay Act of 1963

    A) Mandates equal wages between both genders
    B) Mandates equal wages between the young and aged employees
    C) Mandates equal wages between veterans and civilians
    D) Mandates equal wages between pregnant and non-pregnant women

The correct answer is A:) Mandates equal wages between both genders. The Equal Pay Act of 1963 dictates that a man and women doing comparable jobs should be paid comparable wages.

87) Title VII of the Civil Rights Act does NOT cover discrimination for which of the following

    A) Sex
    B) Race
    C) Sexual preference
    D) Religion

The correct answer is C:) Sexual preference. Title VII of the Civil Rights Act of 1964 prohibits discrimination in hiring, promotion, discharge, pay, fringe benefits, job training, classification, referral, and other aspects of employment, on the basis of race, color, religion, sex or national origin. Homosexuality is NOT a protected class.

88) Sexual harassment is not allowed by what law/agency

    A) EEO
    B) Title VII
    C) ERISA
    D) FMLA

The correct answer is B:) Title VII. Sexual harassment is a form of sex discrimination that violates Title VII of the Civil Rights Act of 1964.

89) If the ABC company has to hire four women to management positions in the next three years, it is participating in

    A) FMLA
    B) Women's rights
    C) Affirmative action
    D) AARP

The correct answer is C:) Affirmative action. Affirmative action plans can be written to include goals/quotas for future hiring practices for protected classes.

90) John is fired for stealing. He _____ eligible for unemployment benefits through unemployment insurance.

    A) Is
    B) Is not
    C) Is, depending on court ruling
    D) None of the above

The correct answer is B:) Is not. Unemployment insurance is a state-by-state mandated program which requires employers to contribute to an unemployment insurance fund. Those who are "justifiably" terminated are not eligible for the benefit.

91) Which of the following is NOT an example of environmental stress?

    A) Traffic
    B) Noise from keyboard
    C) Air pollution
    D) Headache

The correct answer is D:) Headache. Examples of environmental stress are background stressors like air pollution or noise pollution, like when a co-worker is playing his or her radio.

92) _____ has the last word and has the power to complete the settlement.

    A) Mediator
    B) Union leader
    C) Arbitrator
    D) Judge

The correct answer is C:) Arbitrator. An arbitrator also generally has the last word and has the power to complete the settlement.

93) _____ is a neutral third party that helps two parties reach an agreement.

    A) Mediator
    B) Union leader
    C) Arbitrator
    D) Judge

The correct answer is A:) Mediator. A mediator is a neutral third party that helps two parties reach an agreement.

94) Which of the following is a positive type of stress?

A) Distress
B) Eustress
C) Burnout
D) Alarm reaction

The correct answer is B:) Eustress. Although both distress and eustress cause the same body reactions, eustress is considered a positive stress that you get with achievement or meeting your goals and objectives.

95) Which of the following correctly shows the personality types represented by the acronym OCEAN?

A) Affectionate, conscientiousness, extroversion, neuroticism, and openness
B) Extroversion, neuroticism, friendliness, openness, and kindness
C) Conscientiousness, extroversion, agreeableness, neuroticism, and openness
D) Openness, niceness, conscientiousness, extroversion, and agreeableness

The correct answer is C:) Conscientiousness, extroversion, agreeableness, neuroticism, and openness. OCEAN refers to the Big Five personality types.

96) Which of the following deals with unions?

A) NLRB
B) FMLA
C) TQM
D) OSHA

The correct answer is A:) NLRB. The National Labor Relations Board is an independent federal agency to administer the National Labor Relations Act (NLRA), the primary law governing relations between unions and employers in the private sector.

97) When an employee can work from home or wherever they choose it is called

A) Flex time
B) Telecommuting
C) Job sharing
D) Job mentoring

The correct answer is B:) Telecommuting. Telecommuting is when employees can work out of the office, wherever they choose.

98) When a complex set of skills need to be taught to employees, the best approach is

    A) Whole
    B) Module or part
    C) Complete
    D) None of the above

The correct answer is B:) Module or part. When a lot of information needs to be learned, the best approach is in part otherwise known as a module. Each section is taught one at a time, building on the previous section.

99) For what purpose do managers NOT use performance appraisals?

    A) Layoffs
    B) Team selection
    C) Training needs
    D) Human resource planning

The correct answer is D:) Human resource planning. Managers use performance appraisals to determine which employees to terminate, which employees would make good teams and which employees need additional training.

100) Different managers use performance appraisals for different purposes. A developmental manager would use it to determine

    A) Terminations
    B) Training
    C) Promotion
    D) Counseling referral

The correct answer is B:) Training. Managers who are "developing" employees are focused on training. They are also known as training managers.

101) Different managers use performance appraisals for different purposes. A administrative manager would use it to determine

A) Terminations
B) Training
C) Promotion
D) Counseling referral

The correct answer is A:) Terminations. Administrators are concerned with the "big picture" and will use performance information to determine who must be terminated if a downsizing is in the future.

102) When projects are sent outside of the organization for completion it is called

A) Multinational
B) Outsourcing
C) Job sharing
D) Networking

The correct answer is B:) Outsourcing. Outsourcing is finding "sources" outside the company to complete projects or tasks.

103) WARN applies for companies with how many employees?

A) 10
B) 50
C) 100
D) 500

The correct answer is C:) 100. The Worker Adjustment and Retraining Notification Act (WARN) protects workers, their families, and communities by requiring most employers with 100 or more employees to provide notification 60 calendar days in advance of plant closings and mass layoffs.

104) Which of the following is NOT benefit of employee leasing?

   A) Employees cost less in salary
   B) Employers do not pay benefits
   C) Employees can be easily terminated
   D) Increased legal liabilities

The correct answer is D:) Increased legal liabilities. There are less legal liabilities involved in having temporary workers or by using leased employees.

105) What is ergonomics?

   A) The study of people
   B) The study of organizations
   C) The study of people and their surroundings
   D) The study of workspaces and how they interact with people

The correct answer is D:) The study of workspaces and how they interact with people. Ergonomics is the study of how people interact with their desks, computers, etc. The main goal is to eliminate health risks from working at a desk or workstation from strain, etc.

106) If 100 women were interviewed for jobs in a craft store and 20 were hired, according to the 4/5 rule, how many men must be hired if 75 were interviewed?

   A) 4
   B) 8
   C) 10
   D) 12

The correct answer is D:) 12. Do the math carefully, if 20 of 100 women were hired, that results in a of 20%. You can't have a selection rate for the men less than 80% of the women selection rate. 80% of 20% = 16% selection rate minimum. 16% of 75 interviewed = 12.

107) Which of the following is a designated person to mainly hear grievances from employees?

A) Ombudsman
B) Manager
C) Coworker
D) Entrepreneur

The correct answer is A:) Ombdusman. An ombudsman is a designated person to mainly hear grievances from employees.

108) Which of the following includes a neutral third party AND is legally binding?

A) Mediation
B) Arbitration
C) Both mediation and arbitration
D) None of the above

The correct answer is B:) Arbitration. Both mediation and arbitration include neutral third parties but only arbitration is legally binding.

109) When John is unlikely to be able to move up in the company he has reached a

A) Glass ceiling
B) Career plateau
C) Job dissatisfaction
D) Burnout

The correct answer is B:) Career plateau. Career plateau is when a person is unlikely to move up the ladder at their current company.

110) Gloria is an Asian woman working at a large corporation. If she is unable to move up further in the corporation what is the most likely reason?

A) Glass ceiling
B) Career plateau
C) Job dissatisfaction
D) Burnout

The correct answer is A:) Glass ceiling. Glass ceiling is a term that applies to women and minorities. This is an invisible barrier that they are unable to pass due to company culture.

111) Groups of knowledge, policies and culture that give a company its direction and delivers results are called

   A) Contributory plan
   B) Codetermination
   C) Core competencies
   D) Cultural environment

The correct answer is C:) Core competencies. In a training environment, core competencies are the "core" skills or ideas that will make an employee successful.

112) Social security benefits are based on the primary insurance amount, which is formulated using average wage indices and bend points. A COLA increases which of the following?

   A) Bend points
   B) Average wage indices
   C) Primary insurance amount
   D) None of the above

The correct answer is C:) Primary insurance amount. A COLA affects social security benefits.

113) Which of the following is an example of a compressed work week schedule?

   A) Four 8 hour shifts
   B) Four 10 hour shifts
   C) Five 8 hour shifts
   D) Five 10 hour shifts

The correct answer is B:) Four 10 hour shifts. A compressed work week schedule allows an employee works the same amount of hours weekly in less workdays.

114) If Paul's company uses Xerox as an example of where they want to be in the market and how they want to do things, they are using the company as a

   A) Benchmark
   B) Competitor
   C) SWOT
   D) Trend analysis

The correct answer is A:) Benchmark. When a company uses industry leaders as a measurement of where they want to be it is called benchmarking.

115) Which of the following industries is likely to have the LEAST amount of union members?

    A) Actors
    B) Teachers
    C) Automotive workers
    D) Accountants

The correct answer is D:) Accountants. Actors, teachers and automotive workers are generally all part of unions.

116) Which law was the first federal law regulating labor disputes?

    A) Civil Service Reform Act
    B) Taft Hartley Act
    C) Railway Labor Act
    D) None of the above

The correct answer is C:) Railway Labor Act.

117) Which of the following is a function of human resource management?

    A) Performance appraisal
    B) Staffing
    C) Labor relations
    D) All of the above

The correct answer is D:) All of the above. HRM is important to maintaining good working relations in relation to staffing, training and development, performance appraisal, communication and labor relations.

118) Why is human resource management more complex in relation to MNC's?

    A) The distance between headquarters and subsidiaries
    B) Differences between headquarters and subsidiaries
    C) Managing the number of employees from so many different locations
    D) Increased discrimination that occurs in multinational corporations

The correct answer is B:) Differences between headquarters and subsidiaries. Finding policies that work in different situations while trying to maintain quality can be difficult.

119) If an employer is able to terminate you at any time for any reason you are a

    A) Pain
    B) Salaried employee
    C) Contract employee
    D) At-will-employee

The correct answer is D:) At-will-employee. At-will-employees are able to quit at any time and can be terminated at any time and for any reason unless it is a protected class, such as being fired for gender, religion, race, etc.

120) Mary notices that the machine she is working on is broken. She tells her manager who decides not to fix it and continue to use it. This manager is showing

    A) Proactive decision making
    B) Negligence
    C) Good thinking skills
    D) Reasonable care

The correct answer is B:) Negligence. Negligence is knowing when you have a problem and choosing not to fix it, regardless of the circumstances. Negligence is when a company does not give reasonable care to the health and wellbeing of the employees.

121) Who created Theory X and Theory Y?

    A) Max Weber
    B) Abraham Maslow
    C) Douglas McGregor
    D) Frank Gilbreth

The correct answer is C:) Douglas McGregor.

122) John's supervisor doesn't like him. His supervisor tells his team to make things uncomfortable for John by scheduling poor shifts, denying vacation time, makes sure equipment isn't available, even vandalizes his locker and personal effects. John is frustrated and quits because of the working environment. This is called

A) Termination
B) Constructive discharge
C) Pink slip
D) Hazing

The correct answer is B:) Constructive discharge. When a supervisor or company makes a working environment that is completely unreasonable and unfair and an employee quits as a result it is called constructive discharge because the company contributed to the discharge through willful acts. Hazing, while similar, is when you are "tested" by your peers for acceptance into the group, not purposely aggravated into leaving.

123) When unions and human resources meet to achieve better wages, benefits and working conditions, it is known as

A) Collective bargaining
B) Good-faith transactions
C) Negotiations
D) None of the above

The correct answer is A:) Collective bargaining. HR and Unions meet to discuss many aspects of working life.

124) If Peter is found with cocaine in his desk at work the most likely course of action is

A) Counseling
B) Termination
C) Promotion
D) Reprimand

The correct answer is B:) Termination. Most companies have a zero tolerance for illegal drugs in the workplace as they are legally liable when on their property. If it was alcohol that was found, a reprimand and referral to counseling may have been given.

125) Quality circles address problems such as

    A) Safety
    B) Product design
    C) Manufacturing processes
    D) All of the above

The correct answer is D:) All of the above. Quality circles address problems such as safety, product design, and manufacturing processes.

126) Agreeableness is one of the big five personality types. Which of the following is NOT a characteristic of agreeableness?

    A) Friendly
    B) Sensitive
    C) Compassionate
    D) None of the above

The correct answer is B:) Sensitive. Agreeableness describes a person who is trusting, altruistic, kind, affectionate, compassionate, and cooperative. Sensitivity is a characteristic of neuroticism.

127) WARN requires employees to be notified how many days in advance of layoffs?

    A) 7
    B) 21
    C) 30
    D) 60

The correct answer is D:) 60. The Worker Adjustment and Retraining Notification Act (WARN) protects workers, their families, and communities by requiring most employers with 100 or more employees to provide notification 60 calendar days in advance of plant closings and mass layoffs.

128) _____ is when the company wants to reduce its employees to improve the bottom line.

A) Downsizing
B) Outplacement
C) Voluntary turnover
D) Layoff

The correct answer is A:) Downsizing. Downsizing is when the company wants to reduce its employees to improve the bottom line.

129) Mary comes to work without her uniform. Her supervisor sends her directly home. This is an example of her supervisor apply which rule

A) Investigative
B) Discipline status
C) Progressive
D) Hot-stove

The correct answer is D:) Hot-stove. The hot-stove rule is literal. A consequence needs to come right after the infraction, just like the burning sensation comes right after you put your hand on a stove.

130) When Tom is late the first time, he gets a warning. When he is late the second time, he gets written up. If he is late a third time, he is penalized the days pay by being sent home. This is an example of

A) Investigative discipline
B) Discipline status
C) Progressive discipline
D) Hot-stove rule

The correct answer is C:) Progressive discipline. Progressive discipline is when the consequences increase with the incidence rate.

131) When a group of employees want to be represented or are grouped together for bargaining purposes they are called

A) Yellow dog
B) Union
C) Union representation
D) Bargaining unit

The correct answer is D:) Bargaining unit. When a group of employees want to be represented or are grouped together for bargaining purposes they are called bargaining unit.

132) Silvia thinks that she is underpaid and wants a raise. Which of the following would be best to show her manager in support of her position?

A) Job listings
B) Pay grade listing
C) Wage and salary survey
D) Point method report

The correct answer is C:) Wage and salary survey. A wage and salary survey shows comparative wages for positions in a particular area or market.

133) Executive order 11246 enforces

A) Union voting rules
B) Union negotiation rules
C) NLRB agendas
D) Affirmative action

The correct answer is D:) Affirmative action.

134) Incidence rate, the amount of injuries on the worksite, is calculated per _____ full time employees per year.

A) 10
B) 50
C) 100
D) 500

The correct answer is C:) 100. Incidence rate, the amount of injuries on the worksite, is calculated per 100 full time employees per year divided by the total hours worked.

135) The Delphi technique is designed to

    A) Solve problems through group discussion
    B) Create a majority group opinion on a particular topic
    C) Identify key agreements and disagreements on a real-world topic
    D) Analyze all aspects of a situation from multiple points of view

The correct answer is B:) Create a majority group opinion on a particular topic.

136) FEP stands for what

    A) Free enterprise permits
    B) Fair employment practices
    C) Fun entrepreneurship program
    D) Frequent employee perks

The correct answer is B:) Fair employment practices. FEPs or fair employment practices are state laws that govern employees.

137) _____ provides certain employees with up to 12 weeks of unpaid, job-protected leave per year.

    A) EEO
    B) OSHA
    C) FMLA
    D) ERISA

The correct answer is C:) FMLA. The Family and Medical Leave Act (FMLA) provides certain employees with up to 12 weeks of unpaid, job-protected leave per year.

138) The hot stove method of discipline includes which of the following?

    A) A warning
    B) Immediate discipline/consequence
    C) Consistent application
    D) All of the above

The correct answer is D:) All of the above.

139) When an employee is paid by company ABC but works at company PDQ they are involved in

   A) Job sharing
   B) Independent contractor
   C) Flextime
   D) Employee leasing

The correct answer is D:) Employee leasing. Employee leasing and temporary employees are paid by a separate employer than the one they report to during the day.

140) It is illegal to give a candidate a polygraph test unless the job is for

   A) Teacher
   B) Pharmaceutical sales person
   C) Banker
   D) Store clerk

The correct answer is B:) Pharmaceutical sales person. The Employee Polygraph Protection Act of 1988 prohibits the use of polygraph in pre-hire screening except in the case of government agencies, pharmaceutical companies, and security guards.

141) ABC plant closes its offices and plant during a strike this is called a

   A) Buyout
   B) Strike
   C) Arbitration
   D) Lockout

The correct answer is D:) Lockout. A lockout is when an employer closes their plant or offices during a labor strike or union problem.

142) The Delphi method consists of

   A) Surveys
   B) Interviews
   C) Questionnaires
   D) None of the above

The correct answer is C:) Questionnaires. A facilitator sends out questionnaires which pertain to a particular topic, and a group of participants anonymously respond to the questionnaires.

143) An accountant says he is having back pain. He asks his employer for an ergonomic chair. The employee has no obvious disability or known medical condition. His employer asks him to provide documentation from a physician that describes his disability and substantiates his need for an ergonomic chair. According to ergonomics and reasonable accommodation:

A) The employer is not required to provide a new chair because only giving Paul a new chair is favoritism.
B) Because no other accountant has need for an ergonomic chair, it does not fall under the category of reasonable accommodation.
C) The employer is required to provide a new chair with or without the documentation.
D) The employer is only required to provide a new chair with the documentation.

The correct answer is D:) The employer is only required to provide a new chair with the documentation. Because the disability and need for accommodation is not obvious, the employee must provide the documentation or the employer can refuse to provide the chair.

144) In a compressed work week schedule, an employee works a usual 35-40 hour workweek in less than ___ days.

A) 4
B) 5
C) 6
D) 7

The correct answer is B:) 5.

145) Which of the following is a log of work-related injuries and illnesses?

A) Form 100
B) Form 200
C) Form 300
D) Form 400

The correct answer is C:) Form 300. The OSHA Form 300 is a log that contains all work-related injuries and illnesses.

146) When a company is paying the salary that the market demands it is called

    A) Trailing the market
    B) Leading the market
    C) Meeting the market
    D) None of the above

The correct answer is C:) Meeting the market.

147) When an interest in the people's problems affects the outcome, not the changes themselves, it is known as

    A) Hawthorne effect
    B) Taylor effect
    C) Laissez faire effect
    D) Groupthink effect

The correct answer is A:) Hawthorne effect.

148) Executive Order 11246 refers to what?

    A) OHSA
    B) Equal Employment Opportunity
    C) AARP
    D) None of the above

The correct answer is B:) Equal Employment Opportunity.

Test Taking Strategies

Here are some test-taking strategies that are specific to this test and to other DSST tests in general:

- Keep your eyes on the time. Pay attention to how much time you have left.

- Read the entire question and read all the answers. Many questions are not as hard to answer as they may seem. Sometimes, a difficult sounding question really only is asking you how to read an accompanying chart. Chart and graph questions are on most DANTES/DSST tests and should be an easy free point.

- If you don't know the answer immediately, the new computer-based testing lets you mark questions and come back to them later if you have time.

- Read the wording carefully. Some words can give you hints to the right answer. There are no exceptions to an answer when there are words in the question such as always, all or none. If one of the answer choices includes most or some of the right answers, but not all, then that is not the answer. Here is an example:

The primary colors include all of the following:

A) Red, Yellow, Blue, Green

B) Red, Green, Yellow

C) Red, Orange, Yellow

D) Red, Yellow, Blue

Although item A includes all the right answers, it also includes an incorrect answer, making it incorrect. If you didn't read it carefully, were in a hurry, or didn't know the material well, you might fall for this.

- Make a guess on a question that you do not know the answer to. There is no penalty for an incorrect answer. Eliminate the answer choices that you know are incorrect. For example, this will let your guess be a 1 in 3 chance instead.

🎓 *Legal Note*

FLASHCARDS

This section contains flashcards for you to use to further your understanding of the material and test yourself on important concepts, names or dates. Read the term or question then flip the page over to check the answer on the back. Keep in mind that this information may not be covered in the text of the study guide. Take your time to study the flashcards, you will need to know and understand these concepts to pass the test.

Affirmative action	Job description
Mediator	Workweek
Expatriate	Entrepreneur
KSAO	Training

A listing of what a job includes such as tasks, duties and responsibilities.

A detailed plan that a company makes to recruit and advance women and minorities.

A period of 168 hours during 7 consecutive 24 hour periods.

A neutral third party that helps two parties reach an agreement.

A person who starts a business.

A person who is sent to work in a foreign country.

A program built primarily to assist employee development.

A person's knowledge, skills, abilities and other characteristics.

Bargaining unit

Job

Gainsharing plans

Job instruction training

ADEA

ADA

Predictive validity test

Avoiding the risk

A set of related tasks or responsibilities.

A set of employees with similiar views who negotiate as a group.

A step-by-step method of teaching a job.

A sharing of profits among employees and management based on preset formulas.

Americans with Disabilities Act

Age Discrimination in Employment Act of 1967

Avoiding certain industries.

An applicant is tested, hired, then evaluated by their current supervisor.

Environmental Stress

Overtime

Job analysis

Paired comparison method

COBRA

HR MAnager

Employee counseling

Managing diversity

Be paid at a rate of at least one and one-half times the employee's regular rate of pay.

Background noise

Comparing each employee to every other employee in a particular area.

Categorizing exactly what skills and tasks a specific job requires.

Counsel employees, perform administrative functions and create and implement policies.

Comprehensive Omnibus Budget Reconciliation Act

Creating a work environment in which women, minorities and disabled people can succeed.

Available for employees typically offered through a medical plan.

Personnel management

Realistic job preview

EAP

ERISA

Job rotation

EEO

EEOC

Peer appraisal

Describing both benefits
and negative aspects
of a job for potential
employees.

Deals with recruitment,
selection, placement,
training, compensation and
working conditions.

Employee Retirement
Income Security Act of
1974.

Employee Assistance
Program

Equal Employment
Opportunity

Employees are moved
from one department
to another in order to
understand how the
business works.

Evaluations completed by
other employees which are
reviewed by management.

Equal Employment
Opportunity Commission

FLSA	FMLA
Termination	**Factor Comparison**
Unions	**Personnel records**
Arbitrator	**HIPAA**

Family and Medical Leave
Act

Family and Medical Leave
Act

ACE CLEP

For a few predetermined
key jobs, points are allotted
and wage rates for such
key jobs are fixed.

ACE CLEP

Firing an employee.

ACE CLEP

Give all the data in the
application along with
education records, test
scores and other factors.

ACE CLEP

Formal associations of
employees to represent
employees in negotiations
with management.

ACE CLEP

Health Insurance
Portability and
Accountability Act

Has the last word and has
the power to complete the
settlement.

Personnel appraisal

Job relatedness

Job design

Job enrichment

Job enlargement

Selection

Critical incident method

Right to know laws

How essential job tasks
are related to the job.

Helps the employee to
know their strengths,
weaknesses, opportunities
and threats.

Improving employee
satisfaction by
increasing the number of
responsibilities or tasks.

Ideal traits for a position.

Interviewing and hiring.

Increasing the number of
tasks an employee must
complete.

Laws which dictate that
employees must be
informed about potential
hazards of their job.

Keeping a record of an
employee's positive or
negative behavior.

Personnel administration

Norris-LaGuardia Act

Role playing

Labor management

Behaviourally anchored rating scale

Aptitude test

Achievement test

Benchmarking

Made "yellow-dog" contracts (a promise from an employee to not join a union) unenforceable.

Looks into manpower resources, aims at harmonious labor, works to achieve organization goals and keeps records.

Managing of manual workers of an organization.

Managers "pretend" to be in a certain role during training to help them understand both sides of a problem.

Measures a new hire's potential.

Matches rating with employee behavior.

Measuring success based on accepted standards.

Measures what a person already knows.

NLRA

NLRB

OSHA

Team interview

Taft Hartley Act

Piece rate

Escalator clauses

Unemployment insurance

National Labor Relations
Board

National Labor Relations
Act

One applicant meets
with several company
employees at one time.

Occupational Safety &
Health Administration

Paid per piece completed
instead of per hour.

Outlawed for unions the
closed shop, jurisdictional
strikes, and secondary
boycotts.

Provides weekly pay to
employees who lost their
job.

Periodic pay raises based
on market inflation.

Shifting the risk	**Alternation ranking method**
Graphology	**Minimizing the risk**
Industrious relations	**Assuming the risk**
Group interview	**Core skills**

Rates employees as a group from best to worst on a particular area.

Purchasing insurance policies.

Screening employees, utilizing network passwords, etc.

Scientific analysis of your handwriting.

Setting aside enough money to pay for potential losses.

Seeks to bring harmonious relations between labor, management and government.

Skills an employee has which can be applied in many jobs.

Several applicants meet with one or more company representatives.

Eustress	**Resource flexibility**
Defined rights	**Human capital**
Reverse discrimination	**Outplacement**
Board interview	**Ergonomics**

The ability of employees to creatively and successfully complete various jobs.

Stress that we can use positively for our personal growth.

The human resources, such as educated staff, that make the company more valuable.

The clearly stated areas of authority held by management.

The process of helping an old employee find work at a new company.

The practice of giving benefits only to protected or minority groups.

The study of designing more comfortable equipment.

The same as a team interview.

Nepotism	Emplyee development
Vestibule training	Virtual office
Commission	Benefits
Incentive plan	Downsizing

Training

The tendency to hire relatives of current employees.

When an employees works at a remote location as if they were in an office.

Training in an offsite facility that mimics the job environment.

The perks associated with a job.

When employees are paid rewards based on a percentage of their sales.

When the company wants to reduce its employees to improve the bottom line.

When performance is directly linked to pay.

Programmed learning

Coaching

Strike

Job sharing

On the job training

Pregnancy Discrimination Act

WARN

Telecommuting

When the new employee works with the employee they are replacing.

When the employee is taught information, asked questions, and reviews the answers with the trainer.

When two or more people share the same job responsibilities.

When the workers do not come to work until the problem is resolved.

Women affected by pregnancy or related condition must receive equal treatment.

When you learn the job by actually doing it.

Working remotely from the office or from home.

Worker Adjustment and Retraining Notification Act

Made in the USA
Middletown, DE
22 January 2016